When I look back at my life it didn't turn out as I had dreamed it would when I was a little girl. Nor did it turn out as I dreamed as a big girl. Now as an older and much wiser woman I know if you want something to turn out the way you dream… you have to make it happen yourself. That's when family and friends help. No matter what stages of your life you are in, they are always there for you. This may not be the way it is in everyone's life; however, I am truly blessed to have these extraordinary people in mine.

My story starts and ends with sixteen years of an amazing love story that didn't last. For whatever the reasons, I have to believe that it wasn't meant to be and I am now ready to take charge and make the rest of my life the best it can be. It's not easy starting over at any age. However, at 64, who will want me now? I am hoping my young heart and spirit will guide me through the next chapters of my life and starting over again.

No one gets married thinking, "How long will it last"? I felt in my heart, mind and soul that ours would last until the end of time. I had been married before and I honestly thought in my heart and soul that I had finally found "the one".

Now that I'm classified as a "senior" that doesn't mean that I can't take charge and pick up the pieces of my life since being thrown such a curveball. No one said it would be easy; not much in life is. Hopefully we can all learn from our past mistakes and life's valuable lessons. Most of my life has been lived, but it is not too late to make the rest of my life count even more.

With a Flip of a Switch

Carlie Peters

Inspiring Voices®

A Service of **Guideposts**

The names and places have been changed to protect identity. However, this is a true story. My story.

Inspiring Voices books may be ordered through booksellers or by contacting:

Inspiring Voices
1663 Liberty Drive
Bloomington, IN 47403
www.inspiringvoices.com
1-(866) 697-5313

ISBN: 978-1-4624-0265-6 (e)
ISBN: 978-1-4624-0266-3 (sc)

Library of Congress Control Number: 2012913771

Printed in the United States of America

Inspiring Voices rev. date: 9/26/2012

Dedicated to

Any man or woman that has experienced a love that dissolved without explanation and which changed the course of their life forever.

Special Mentions

My sons and daughters-in-law for their wisdom, strength and understanding

My best friend Rachel for all her help and advice for the book

My best friend Addison for her computer expertise

My best friend Marlo for being there 24/7

My brother for changing his lifestyle to accommodate mine

Table of Contents

Foreword

<u>Forgiveness</u>

Anyone can hold a grudge, but it takes a person with character to forgive. When you forgive, you release yourself from a painful burden. Forgiveness doesn't mean what happened was okay, and it doesn't mean that person should still be welcome in your life. It just means that you have made peace with the pain and are ready to let go and move on.

Will you still want me; will you still need me, when I'm Sixty-Four?

Preface

In my lifetime I have been lucky enough to live on three major bays in our beautiful United States. The Chesapeake Bay, Tampa Bay, and the San Francisco Bay. The latter was where I had planned to live out the last few chapters of my life. As circumstances would have it, things changed and I am now back to the Chesapeake Bay to start my new life as a single woman once again. I have come full circle. All three of these bays have played a major part in my life and the bridges that cross them remind me of the journey I am now about to take.

At first it was therapeutic to write a journal of what I was going through. I would wonder how many other wives or husbands had been dealt the same hand as I. I knew on January 1st, 2011 that it would become something more than notes on my tablet. I knew on that New Year's Day that it was time to sit and tell my story.

Friends

Friend: To me, a true friend is there for you no matter what. They don't lie to you. They keep their promises and don't stab you in the back. Let's talk about friends versus acquaintances. Stop and think about whom you consider a true friend: Someone that has your back at all times. Someone you can trust with your life/kids/secrets/money/ integrity. Someone that would drop everything in a minute to help, no questions asked. Someone who would never judge you. Someone who is there through bad times and good times, plus so much more. This is my definition of a true friend.

Count on your fingers and see how many people you know fit this description. We all know a lot of people through the years that we meet at work, school, sports, volunteering, clubs, social networks, and so many people we come across in our everyday life. These are acquaintances, we all have them. They are good sources in our everyday life. This doesn't mean we can't enjoy their company, spend time with them, watch their kids, etc., it's just that these people don't know us the way our true friends do. These are not the people that would necessarily be there for us when times get tough. I am not discounting any person, man or woman; I have met and become friendly with as "acquaintances". But when I finally sat down to write my story, so many things were going thru my head and I didn't know where to begin. So I sat back, took a breath and looked at my surroundings. There was never a time in my life that any of these true friends, who I mention throughout this book, were not there for me. Some of these ladies I've known for years from the very beginning and others along the way. These wonderful friends helped me keep it together, pick myself up, stand tall, be a better person, and do something I always wanted to do, write about my life. I knew someday I would write a book. I wasn't exactly sure what it would entail. It wasn't until recently when I went through this extraordinary life changing experience did the timing now seem appropriate.

So as I began this journey, I asked myself, "Why do I want to share my story"? It is simple; because what I have recently experienced I know others out there have also. And it is my hope that by sharing my story that others won't feel all alone in their experience and that they will feel inspired and realize that what they are going through or have been through will make them stronger if they just believe in themselves.

San Francisco... the Beginning

In the fall of 1993 my BFF Rachel and I traveled to San Francisco to visit my oldest son for a week. Rachel and I always enjoyed a good road trip and this one was bound to be as amazing as the others we had traveled. Never in my wildest dreams did I ever expect to fall in love with "the city by the bay". First and foremost, the weather was absolutely gorgeous. The city itself was an extraordinary display of lights at night and a busy, bustling business district by day. The culture and ambiance was refreshing and the people were like none I had ever encountered before. The idea of being in such a wonderful city was intriguing enough, but the fact that within a short drive you could be at so many diverse environments like the beach, the mountains, Napa Valley or Lake Tahoe, well that was the icing on the cake for me. My son and his friends showed Rachel and me a great time, that's for sure. We frequented many delicious restaurants and the typical tourist attractions like Alcatraz, Pier 39, Lombard

Street, Ghirardelli Square, Muir Woods and of course, the amazing Golden Gate Bridge. The scenery from the many views of the bay was breathtaking.

On our last morning there, Rachel and I shared coffee and pastries while sitting by the bay with the Golden Gate Bridge slightly clouded in fog in the background. I had decided right then and there this was where I wanted to live out the rest of my life. Upon returning to Tampa, I immediately began the process of packing my belongings and planning my move to the west coast. My proverbial nest was empty. I was single and my youngest two sons had moved out to go to college and work. Earlier that year I had ended an intense, two-year relationship with a younger man who had lied to me the whole time about being separated from his wife. So there was nothing to keep me there.

In May of 1994 a friend from San Francisco flew to Tampa to move me out to the west coast. As difficult as it was to leave my two sons and best friend, I knew in my heart this journey was the right thing for me at this time in my life. Even though I was scared to be moving so far away to an unfamiliar city and did not have a job or even a place to live yet, I felt brave at the same time for taking on this life-changing adventure. I was both sad and excited at the same time. Rachel came over the evening before I was to leave. It was bittersweet. She was so excited for me, yet we knew how hard it was going to be to say goodbye. Rachel is 18 years younger than me, but we are bound together in a way like no other. She is like the sister and daughter I never had. There are things the two of us have shared that no one else knows and never will.

We shared two bottles of champagne that night to try and help numb the heartache of saying goodbye. As the evening grew late, we locked ourselves in the bathroom for some privacy. We were like giggly teenagers, yet the tears started to flow as well. As silly as it sounds, Rachel thought we should prick our fingers and become blood sisters. Now, this idea was in part due to the "numb brains" we had at the moment. But it was fitting and neither of us hesitated. So there we stood, two grown women, hugging and crying and holding a tissue on bleeding fingers.

The next morning was even more difficult for me. My youngest son was in north Florida at college and we had seen each other prior to the move. But just before we pulled out of Tampa, we stopped by the restaurant where my middle son was working so I could say goodbye to him. I will never forget looking in the side view mirror of the moving truck as we pulled away and seeing my boy sitting on an air conditioner unit hunched over crying. I almost backed out of the whole thing. But I knew how close my relationship was with my boys and that we would be seeing each other often. And they were happy for me that I was moving to San Francisco and would be living close to my oldest son now. They were proud of me for making such a big change in my life and I had their full support.

Upon arriving to San Francisco I stayed with the friend who moved me out while I looked for work. A few weeks after finding a job I settled into my own apartment. It was perfect! It had beautiful bay windows and many vintage architectural designs that were classic to the older San Francisco buildings.

True love doesn't happen to everyone and if it does there is nothing that can compare. I found that with him. I met Dick in June 1994 in San Francisco. It was my first day on a new job working at a very complex software firm. I was nervous and intimidated by the sophistication of the big city. I had just arrived from Tampa, so talk about going from one extreme to the other. The ladies in the office were okay towards me. I looked very different. Coming from Florida my hair was very blonde and my tan was real. They seemed pale and all wore dark sleek colors like black, brown, grey and taupe. I wore bright colors with lots of flowers and patterns. I was sitting at my desk when Dick walked into my office. He took the time to welcome me and immediately took my mind off those first day jitters. I was instantly at ease with him and the genuine warmth he generated. He did not live in San Francisco but commuted for work from the Midwest. Back then he was a tall, geeky, nice guy with a naïveté' about him that just made him likeable. I knew from that first meeting that we would become friends for life. I could tell from the start how incredibly smart he was. He always asked a lot of questions but never volunteered anything about himself. Does this sound familiar? Needless to say the attraction between us was undeniable, although we kept it to ourselves and did not act on it in any way.

We started talking on the phone every day about everything and anything. There was such a relaxed aura between us and we never had a problem holding conversations. The laughter was abundant. He was good at keeping his private life to himself. Like I said, he could ask me questions but he never revealed too much personal information about himself. Even when I would ask him questions he would be vague and tap dance around an answer. About a month into our friendship he finally revealed to me that he was married with two young sons.

As time passed, our friendship grew stronger every day and after about six months I could feel myself falling in love with him. I never expressed these feelings to him as I was not sure he felt the same. I was single and had nothing to lose. He on the other hand had so much more at stake. I told him there was no way I could get intimately involved with a married man and that we would have to remain platonic friends. I had already been there and done that and I wasn't about to go down that painful path again.

He commuted for work back then coming to the bay area a couple times a month. We continued with our platonic friendship and after a few months he told me his marriage was over. I remember him coming back from being with his family and bringing boxes and boxes of computer equipment and books. He told me he had separated from his wife and was moving to the west coast and wanted to be with me. We had been friends for several months at that point and we felt very close to one another. We became lovers and he moved into my apartment. That was the start of the love story we shared.

I was older than him and that bothered me. However, it didn't seem to bother him. People have always told me I look a lot younger than I am and I have a very youthful attitude and vibrant personality. We laughed a lot back in the beginning as new couples do. Sex was plentiful and we just got along and we really liked each other. We talked for hours and hours, never running out of anything to say. Then we would have hours of just sitting in silence. It was enough just being together. We were falling madly in love every day. I had never met anyone like him. My friends didn't understand what we were all about until each of them spent time with us and could see and feel the love we shared. It was as real as it gets. For me anyhow. I felt overpowering trust in him and he in me.

I can't say it enough; he was one of the smartest people I had ever met. Book smart, not people or street smart. That's where I come in. We balanced each other out. He was the first man that had made me feel really good about myself in a long, long time. He was sincere, honest, warm, weird, educated, and so much more. We loved each other from the bottom of our hearts and it radiated to those who knew us. People would say when they thought of the ideal couple they thought of us. We did have a significant age difference between us that most couples would have shied away from. The age difference no longer bothered me. We loved each other for whom we were, not how old we were.

He wasn't at all what you would call a romantic man, but he did have his own special way of making something like writing on a sticky note, "you are my all-time favorite girl", seem so meaningful. He didn't like giving gifts at Christmas, birthdays, anniversaries or Valentine's Day. He would always ask, "Why does one have to prove their love because it's a certain day of the year"? There was a part of me that had to agree with him.

Our favorite thing to do was to walk or sit by the Golden Gate Bridge. We would hold each other close while gazing at that beautiful structure. No matter what time of day the view was spectacular! I could never get enough of its beauty. It made perfect sense for us to get engaged mid span one cold, foggy night in October 1995. I was sitting at home in our cozy, warm flat watching television while Dick was in his office working, as he always was. He came out from his office and insisted we bundle up and take a walk across the bridge. It was late and I didn't want to leave the warmth of our home to take a walk in the cold. But he was very insistent, so I gave in. Thirty minutes later we had walked halfway across the most beautiful bridge in the world and in the background the city was lit up like a fairy tale. It was a perfect setting. He took a small black box out of his pocket and handed it to me to open. It was empty! He took off his glove and the ring was on his pinky finger. He then slipped it on the ring finger of my left hand and said it was my "sweetie" ring. That's how he was. My heart was bursting with love for this man. I was floating on cloud nine and everyone noticed.

In Sickness and in Health

He was prone to throat infections that were so severe he eventually had his tonsils removed in 1996. As an adult this operation isn't as easy as it is when you are a child. However, it was like dealing with a child the day we checked into the hospital in San Francisco. First of all, he isn't the easiest person to get along on any given day under any circumstance, so you can imagine his behavior when he was stripped of his belongings and given a hospital gown. A hospital gown? That was not even an option in his mind. What did he think he was going to wear? When he was asked to remove his underwear he would not do it. No way. They finally came in and gave him the shot to calm him down before entering the operating room. At that point he was driving everyone around him nuts! We all deserved a medal having to witness this grown man behaving like a three year old. Off he went down the hall still jabbering about keeping his drawers on through surgery and how he didn't want anyone looking at his "parts". Now you know if someone made a big stink like he did that as soon as that anesthesia kicked in everyone would take a peek, just to see what all the fuss was about.

It was a long operation for a tonsillectomy. Needless to say as crazy as he drove me before the surgery, I was worried sick. Finally, after three hours his surgeon came and told me there had been a complication. He coughed in the recovery room and popped the stitches. They had to immediately return to the operating room and re-stitch the incisions again. He came out of recovery and they kept him overnight, so of course I stayed all night with him. He was released the next day and told to take it easy for a week. But of course being a stubborn man, he decided he was well enough to go back to work sooner than he was advised to do so.

He was back at work for only one day when he started to hemorrhage. Off to the hospital emergency room we go. He was losing a lot of blood when we arrived and they took him in right away for emergency surgery. I remember sitting in the waiting room all night by myself rocking back and forth thinking what I would do if something happened to him. The doctors and nurses would come out and give me updates saying, "We are doing everything we can", and that's not what I wanted to hear. I wanted to hear he was going to be alright. This is when I knew how much I loved this man; the thought of losing him was not an option. Finally the news I was waiting for. He was out of surgery and they had stopped the bleeding.

It was touch and go, the surgeon said. He had lost 17% of his blood supply. The doctor came out and escorted me back to the recovery room. I wasn't quite prepared for the sight I was about to see. He had a huge bandage on his neck where the incision was made to stop the bleeding, he had a tampon up each nostril to stop the nosebleed, he had tubes in his arms and his hair was sticking straight up in the air… still not sure how that happened. To make things worse, he had a catheter put in during surgery. So when they pulled it out all he could yell was "my dick hurts, my dick hurts" over and over again. Oh dear God! His doctor was in the room writing in her chart and said in her sweet voice, "I love it when they come out of anesthesia; their true personality really comes out". The finale of this long night came when a very nice gay gentleman entered the recovery room to take blood from this creature from another planet. The verbiage that came from his mouth was utterly shocking and vulgar. "GET THIS COCKSUCKER AWAY FROM ME". This lovely male nurse just smiled at me and responded, "I've been called worse". It was then that the nurse administered a magic needle into his IV and immediately there was silence. Hallelujah! There would be peace and quiet for awhile. Needless to say no one spoke a word, but they all just looked at me sympathetically and at one another in relief and just smiled.

He was in the hospital for days. I was working full time each day and then spending my evenings at the hospital. I remember he wanted me to bring him orange popsicles after I left work to come see him on my nightly visit. Not every corner store in San Francisco sells orange popsicles. After visiting multiple stores with no luck finding these damn orange popsicles, I bought him his favorite brand of vanilla ice cream. He made such a fuss because there were no orange popsicles. He went on and on about it for days making snide comments that I couldn't even manage to get them. I should have known then how selfish this man could be. He still tells that story making me feel like I failed him in some way. I remember having to fix liver and onions, anything that had iron in it. He had to build back his blood supply and eating healthy was a must. I bent over backwards making sure he was comfortable. He never was a good sick person and just wanted to be left alone. That worked for me!

There were many other times he would suffer from severe throat infections or stomach problems and I would get him whatever he needed to make him comfortable. But like I said, he would rather be alone when he was sick.

Since we have been together I have had my share of medical issues, this is where we are all different. Unlike him, I welcome a cup of tea or someone helping me if I need it. He doesn't like sick people so he keeps his distance. It was usually one of my dear girlfriends who would come over to care for me when I was sick. And without saying so, I knew deep down he was relieved they did because it let him off the hook.

Proposal... Marriage

It was November 1996 and I was at work when he called and asked me if I wanted to go see Elvis. I jokingly asked him if he was drinking. He said no and asked me if I wanted the same last name as his. This was his way of proposing.

It was a beautiful sunny day when we arrived in Las Vegas on December 7, 1996. We rented a car and drove straight to the courthouse to get our marriage license. There were at least twenty other couples doing the same thing. Some were in bridal gowns and tuxedos and some wore jeans and t-shirts. You saw anything and everything. Our appointment at The Chapel of the Bells was for noon. We arrived fifteen minutes early. There were a few rows of pews, the pulpit for the reverend and lots of silk flowers displayed all around. It was lovely. I wore a beautiful Giorgio Armani red pant suit that I had bought for my birthday. It was the most expensive piece of clothing I had ever bought and it was stunning. Dick was wearing a blue suit and bought me a beautiful silk flower bouquet. The only ones in the chapel then was the minister, his wife and the two of us. We signed the paperwork and gave the camera to the minister's wife and walked down the ten foot isle and became husband and wife. It was no fuss, no muss.

We left the chapel before 12:30pm and headed over to Caesar's Palace where we had a lovely lunch. After lunch we walked through the Forum at Caesar's to buy a pair of tennis shoes. My feet were killing me from wearing heels. Our flight back to San Francisco wasn't for a few hours so we decided to take a tour of the Hoover Dam. Talk about a spectacular, interesting and not to mention breathtaking experience. We both enjoyed it and found every minute of the tour and the beauty of the dam to be the icing on the cake for our special day. A day I knew I would always cherish. Each time we did something like this or experienced something new together, we fell more deeply in love.

Prior to our wedding we knew his job was sending us to the east coast. The day after we were married we flew back east to Virginia to begin our life as husband and wife.

When we finally arrived on the east coast the apartment we were going to rent wasn't ready for us to move into due to delays in construction because of severe weather. My friend Addison put up with two roommates for almost three months. That is a true test of friendship... living together. Our apartment was close to the train, which was my means of transportation to and from work. We arrived from the west coast with only one car and we were now living in the suburbs. As great as it was to be back on home soil and to be around family and friends, I longed to move back to San Francisco where I had truly left my heart. After a year of working on the east coast Dick's job brought us back to the San Francisco Bay area. This is where our life truly began.

The Good Years

In late '97 when we finally got back to California there were no apartments available in the city. Everywhere you went there was a waiting list and bidding wars to get in. We moved to the east bay for six months before finally finding a flat back in the city. Not quite as nice as the one we left, but it was ok. I was just thankful to be back in my city by the bay. Dick decided law school was the next career path he wanted to pursue. So pursue it he did. Anything Dick wanted, Dick got; especially if it was for himself. I had taken a wonderful job that I loved in the city and was at work every day at 5:30am. The hours were brutal but it didn't seem to be an issue as I was happy and he was happy. We didn't see a lot of each other because he was still working part time during the day and going to law school at night. My work hours had me in bed by 9pm and waking up at 4:00am. And because of my work schedule and his class and work schedules, he was coming in the door each night around 9pm as I was going to bed. The time we did have together was special; we laughed a lot, enjoying every minute living in our magical city together. Quality over quantity we would always say. We knew that our patience would pay off one day once he was finished with school and had his law degree and began his career as an attorney.

During this time we walked the city from east to west, north to south. When we weren't walking we would take his motorcycle on the 49-mile tour or ride up into the Marin Headlands. The time we spent together was blissful. He was my best friend.

During the years we lived in San Francisco he was always working on some kind of degree or test. He was determined to pass every class and test and always did. I don't know if he felt like he would be more of a man to have all these degrees on his wall and I never could understand it. It was like he had something to prove to himself. All I know is he was always studying for some test and every course or test he took cost us money. His student loan payments weren't cheap either. I had mixed emotions about him attending law school and he certainly didn't like when I called him a "diploma junkie". He literally held more degrees than most doctors. His mind was like a sponge and he could never learn enough. Education seemed an obsession with him. I guess this is a good thing.

When I first heard he was going to take the LSAT's for Law School, I knew he would have his head buried in books for the next three plus years. He could only work no more than twenty hours a week in order to attend law school in the evenings. One thing for sure, when he was focused on something he wanted he gave it 110%. That's how he did things and this next degree would be no exception.

He passed the California State Bar and his choice of Law was Intellectual Property Rights. He had chosen that direction when the dot-commers were in full bloom. His goal was to be the attorney for a new up and coming startup Dot-com Company. After that went south he decided to give a law firm two years before going out on his own. He did just that.

With his multiple degrees in technology and his recent law degree, he could pick and choose. So he chose to go into real estate since that market was booming. Once again, he went to school and obtained his real estate broker's license. He sold several homes the first year in this new career venture and the next two years were spent helping clients with refinancing. We met a lot of nice folks during the few years he was doing the real estate gig. I was working with him out of my office in the house. I would listen to him talking with his clients. He had such a genuine, kind, soft, caring way of communicating with these people. I believed every word he said, as did they. Business was good for two years. We paid our bills, made money and spent money, never saving a dime. We were extremely happy back then. We traveled to Las Vegas every year for a convention and took many vacations. I was able to travel to the east coast to visit my family and Rachel in Tampa whenever possible. His boys would visit us in California. Things were good.

Our relationship was stronger than ever. I felt closer to him than I ever had before. With the exception of an occasional financial issue that caused a few arguments between us, everything was blissful. With Dick's knowledge of real estate we decided it was time to move out of the city as it was getting more and more expensive to live there and we needed to invest in a home for ourselves instead of throwing away our money every month on rent. It was 2001. I was hesitant at first. How could I leave the city I adored so much? The culture and arts and my friends? But he was right. We were throwing money down the drain on rent.

So after much searching, we settled on Sausalito, just across the Golden Gate Bridge. The distance wasn't so bad and my commute to work was beautiful crossing that amazing bridge every day. Dick continued to work out of the house in real estate. This was our dream house. We built her from the ground up and because Dick didn't care nor have the patience or desire to be involved, I designed and chose every little detail myself and he trusted me to do it all. During the building process we would cross the bridge weekly from the city to take progress pictures. I continued to meet with the builders on a regular basis to choose the fixtures, flooring, paint colors and cabinets. Because of how involved I was in choosing every detail, the vision in my head was quite vivid and upon completion I was in awe. I couldn't wait to move into our new home and continue our blissful life together. The house was complete in 2002. Together we chose all the new furniture to go with the French Country decor, it was lovely when it all came together. It was warm, cheerful and inviting. The house wrapped its arms around you the moment you walked through the front doors. It was a beautiful two-story, 2,200 square foot home with four bedrooms, two and a half baths and a two-car garage. The back courtyard had a large, bricked patio with high privacy walls and included beautiful landscaping with shrubs, bright blooming flowers, a maple tree, and a huge fountain that sat in the corner. The sound of the water flowing through the three-tiered fountain was relaxing and heavenly. The impeccable year-round climate for spending time outside was perfect and once we added a grill we spent almost every evening eating on the patio. We entertained regularly with close friends and family joining us for special gatherings and holidays. We were social drinkers and indulged in great wines and champagne when we entertained. I was such a social butterfly and loved hosting these dinner parties and gatherings.

Our social life in Sausalito revolved around many activities and we had a vast amount of acquaintances and a few very close friends. Dick met so many people through business and networked all the time. One of the main reasons I loved the San Francisco area was because there was always something going on; festivals, art fairs, concerts in the park, parades. The weather was always beautiful and we enjoyed going to these events as much as we could.

After a couple of years we added to our family a beautiful black Persian cat. As cheesy as it may sound, the name "Fluffy" was fitting for this ball of fur. Dick was actually the one who picked out Fluffy and we all bonded immediately. One happy little family!

So yes, we were now living in our own little slice of heaven and even on rainy days I felt the sunshine all around me. It was the warmth and feeling of contentment that was shining through my heart. I felt safe and secure and was the happiest I had ever been in my life. This happiness continued for a few years as we continued to enjoy traveling to great destinations like Puerto Rico, Hawaii, Mexico and New York City. Our life together was beyond storybook.

Dick was successful earning a decent living and because of the health issues I was experiencing it was time for me to quit my job in May of 2005. I had been diagnosed with early stage lupus back in 1999 and was beginning to experience more symptoms of tiredness, joint pain, etc. I welcomed retirement although I was heartbroken to leave my boss and co-workers at the company where I had worked for over six years. My boss treated me like royalty and spoiled me with business trips and bonuses for all my hard work. We were very close and telling him I was leaving was very sad indeed. Although I was officially retired from the work force, I would work from home for Dick's business for the next two years.

In June of '05 I read in our local paper that there was going to be a performance from one of the local dance theaters. It was being held at the high school not far from our house.

It was a warm Friday night as I walked to the school, took my seat in the audience and watched as the curtain went up and the magic began. The dancers ranged from three years old to adults, boys, girls, ladies and men. I sat and watched remembering back when I was four years old dancing on stage for the first time. It brought back such warm memories. As the dancers performed their numbers I noticed they all looked like they really enjoyed being on that stage. The final number was the turning point for me. The adult ladies came on stage and I noticed this one lovely lady, my age, jumping, kicking, spinning, and tapping just owning that stage. I said to myself that night I would be on that stage next year. And I was.

In September I started my classes with the instructor Ms. D. One of the lupus-related medical conditions I have is a joint issue and dancing has helped me more than any physical therapy. I'm not saying it hasn't been without injuries, especially on my back and knees. Dancing helped get my arms, legs and hips moving again. I was like an old car that hadn't been driven in a while; I needed a jump start and lubrication. That can be taken a couple of ways! Some nights I would be so sore when I got home I had ice on my knee and heat on my back, but it was worth every shuffle ball change. Of course the one element I somehow keep forgetting, I'm not twenty anymore!

The people I met through dance will always hold a special place in my heart. It was a fun time and it was my time for me. Our group had a great chemistry and even though some dancers left and new ones started, no matter who was on the floor we all got along. I know it was because of Ms. D and Jessica. They are amazing instructors and we all loved them.

It was through this dance studio that I met and befriended Marlo. We are the same age and have been best friends ever since. Dick and I became friends with Marlo and her friend Dave. He and Dick got along well and we spent a lot of time socializing with them and having get-togethers on a regular basis.

We had also discovered an amazing local Mexican restaurant that quickly became our favorite place to go. Their margaritas were off the charts delicious and the food was amazing. A lot of our local friends gathered there on a weekly basis to catch up with everyone and enjoy the ambiance and atmosphere. We knew all the employees and they knew us. It was like our own little "Cheers"; where everybody knew your name.

My life was full and always busy. This was retirement? Throughout my entire relationship with Dick I was always the dutiful girlfriend/wife. I took care of EVERYTHING! The household, the cleaning, laundry, shopping, cooking. I even took care of the car maintenance and related issues. The lawn maintenance, household and appliance repairs… you name it. I kept up with our social calendar and made sure we were always in attendance at the right events at the right time for him to network and socialize. When Dick came home from working his dinner was always hot and ready to be served. I waited on him hand and foot. Each morning I would make sure his clothes were ironed and laid out for him. All the way down to his socks and shoes.

In mid-2005 we got the first of two Pugs. Mrs. Ellie was the cutest little thing I had ever seen. We had friends who bred their Pugs and we watched the delivery of our newest baby. Dick was not keen on the whole idea of getting a dog. But I always knew that once I was not working I wanted a dog and I had always favored Pugs. Once Dick saw her at birth he melted and knew she was the one. We both immediately bonded with this bundle of sweetness, but Dick was like a kid. He would lie on the floor and let Mrs. Ellie roll all over him and he would even sleep with her cuddled in his jacket.

A Mother's Advice

The most important person in my life was my mother. She always told me to trust your first instinct. She was always on target when it came to judging people. When my brother or I would bring a new friend home she could tell immediately if that person was okay for us to hang out with. It didn't take us long to realize she was always right. Something a teenage son or daughter never wants to admit about their parents at the time.

That instinct worked very well for me when I became a mother myself. I could tell as soon as one of my boys came home with someone who was trouble. An antenna would go up and I could sense it right away. Same with other people in general. As we get older I think we all get a lot wiser and learn to trust our own instincts. My instincts are sharper now more than ever!

It didn't take me long to see the change coming after he went into business with "her".

I could sense the calm before the storm.

The Beginning of the End

In 2008 the real estate market was now beginning its downturn. Dick had met many people in the real estate industry and it was through these contacts that he was introduced to Puki. She latched onto him like a fly on cow shit! She knew a good business head like his and all his licenses could only bring her more success and money. In mid 2008 he began consulting for her company on a part time basis while still trying to make a living with his real estate business. I sensed a change in him right away. Every night when he came home all he could talk about was Puki this and Puki that. How wonderful and smart she was and blah, blah, blah. He was incessantly speaking of her, I got the impression he literally thought she hung the moon. He raved on and on about her moving to this country and raising a family while working and having a business of her own. Now hold on just a minute! I raised three wonderful, successful sons basically all by myself while working full time. He seemed to have forgotten about that. He acted as if she was the only woman to ever do that.

Then the proverbial "straw that broke the camel's back" came in late 2008 when he went into a business partnership with her without even discussing it with me at all. He told me about it after the fact and after they had signed and filed all the partnership paperwork. He had started packing items in boxes one day from his home office and when I asked him what he was doing he blurted out the news to me about the new partnership and how he was moving into her business office. Are you kidding me? You could have knocked me over with a feather! I was in shock at how he blatantly disregarded and disrespected me in making this kind of huge decision without involving me and I was just as hurt as I was shocked.

The day I met Puki for the first time had a very sad start and ended in a screaming match with him. It was January 2009 and a very dear former coworker was gravely ill and her husband and friends arranged a get together at her home, knowing this would most likely be the last time we were all together with her. It was bittersweet though, seeing how she had become so frail and thin as if it was just an outline of her sitting with us. Hopefully she still understood all the stories we each told of the good old days. It seemed as if she did.

At the end of our visit we drove a good friend back to the city. From there we drove another hour to an eight-year old's birthday party at a pizza venue that catered to kids' birthdays on a Saturday! It wasn't enough to have just been through what was probably the last visit with a dear coworker, but now we are at the noisiest venue in northern California completely surrounded by a huge mass of screaming child monsters jacked up on soda, cake and iced cream and also their stressed out, screaming parents! Something I wouldn't wish on anyone, especially after the sadness we had just left.

This is my first encounter with his new business partner. Dick had felt obligated to accept Puki's invitation to her child's birthday party. When we arrived at the party I saw her right away. You could tell she had been anxiously watching the entrance door for him. As we approached her this woman looked me over like I was a piece of cheap clothing at a yard sale. They took a seat next to one another in a booth leaving me all by myself across from them on the other side while she interrogated me like I was on the witness stand for a crime. It took all the strength I had not to come across the table and slap her. Or him for that matter! The little shoulder bumps and private jokes between them made me want to throw up in their faces. That he could subject me to this after the sad afternoon we just spent was so inconsiderate. Then for him to sit there next to her while she asked me all kinds of personal questions. I almost lost it! I knew nothing about her, especially anything personal, and here she was interrogating me like she knew me. Being the lady I am, I waited until we were on our way home when he asked me, "why so quiet"? If he wasn't driving MY car I would have slapped him right across his smug face!

This is what I mean by stupid. He saw nothing wrong with the way they both treated me, like I was the hired help. I knew from that moment on I didn't like her, trust her or want any part of him and her working together. He started the partnership with her in October 2008. Things were never the same again!

He never said much about the office after that. Their business catered to people who were in the foreclosure process and they helped them obtain loan modifications, among other services. He knew I didn't like him working there, but it paid the bills. I thought from the very beginning she was just using his brains, law degree and security licenses to do what she needed to make the business successful so money could come in for her. Something just didn't sit right. Dick had always been an extremely private person and she knew way too much about our personal life. She was in our business and had a way of getting personal information from him. The man who would have never shared personal information about himself to anyone before had somehow begun to open up to her, of all people! I'm not sure what kind of voodoo spell she used, but somehow she had a way of getting him to confide in her. It made me sick that he was falling for all this. The entire office was mostly her culture except for Dick and a couple of other employees. If someone was hired and took his attention away from her, they would be gone immediately. Once again, more arguments prevailed thereafter. I felt him being pulled away. The more things I would say about her and try to get him to see what I saw in her, the more he would distance himself away from me. He criticized my "so-called instincts" for people and discounted my feelings entirely. The only clients he liked representing were the ones from her ethnic group she would lure into the business. It made him feel superior and she loved it! He loved it too. He was becoming a bully to these poor people on the verge of losing their homes. He loved the power it gave him and the attention she showered on him for it. One afternoon at his request I met him at the office as we were going to leave directly from there to go to an event. I sat in his conference room while waiting for him to finish his work and was appalled to hear how he spoke to his clients. Who was this man?

Puki's husband, the poor guy, works in the office as the "go to errand guy". I had actually met him before I met her. He had stopped by the house once to pick up a lock box. He had a good firm handshake and an honest face. Much different than his wife's. I met him again at the unforgettable child's birthday party where she had introduced him to me as her "man slave". Do I need to say anything more about this woman? I know her husband isn't stupid, but working in the office with his wife and my husband he had to see the way she looks and acts when they were together; which is twelve hours a day, seven days a week. My friend Marlo saw it too when we stopped by his office one Saturday. Puki hangs on Dick's every word. Both his heads are so big he can hardly get through the front door. If his ego wasn't off the charts before, it sure as hell is now. They call him

"Attorney" with almost worship-like admiration and he loves it. As a child and young man he never received any praise for who he was or what he did. I guess all my years of encouragement, support and praise wasn't enough. This group he is now calling "his family", "his people", give him what he needs in that department.

She referred to me as Princess on more than one occasion. In fact one Saturday I stopped by the office to visit him since I never see him at home. It was an hour we could spend together having lunch. I was trying my best to make every attempt to prove to him how much I loved him and still wanted our marriage. As we were leaving she smugly looked me in the eye and asked me, "Do you know what we all call you here"? I turned around unenthusiastically and said, "What"? She said, "Princess". I sparred immediately back at her with confidence, "I've been called worse" and walked right out the door! Again, I wanted to slap her across that ugly, mean, nasty face of hers. Ask me… where was he while this was being said? He was right smack behind me, never saying a word. He let her humiliate me and we walked out the door. I asked why he didn't have my back, why he let her get away with being so disrespectful to me, and his response was, "She was just joking". Ummm… NO SHE WASN'T! There he is… stupid again! He has blinders on when it comes to that group and I swear he has been brainwashed and nothing will make me ever think different. She and the whole bunch have been a thorn in my side since he stepped foot inside the office and became partners with her. They never once treated me with any respect. He is a different person. Not the fun-loving, wonderful man he was when we met and married. It is true, people change. His change is not for the good. I can't let him or his work peers bring me down any longer. If he doesn't want to be with me, he gets his wish!

The entire time all this was going on, my family and friends were there to get me through the arguments and be with me through the long nights of being alone. Our friends and family could see the drastic change in Dick's behavior and demeanor. I tried to keep things the way they were at home; it just was never the same once he started working and spending time with "his people". I did everything I could to please him and try to keep our home life and marriage together and he resented me for not liking them. How could I "like" them? They were taking away the man I had fallen so deeply in love with. I bit my tongue more times than I cared only to keep the peace between us. I was trying, but he was making it increasingly more difficult for me to be civil much longer. I was getting nothing in return except more grief. If he wasn't going to bother acknowledging the negative changes in him and was going to continue to mistreat me and leave me behind, then what else could I do? I was slowly becoming a "party of one".

How did things get to this point? Why couldn't he see the drastic changes in himself and our relationship? Dick began working very long hours and was out the door early every morning and never home at night until usually after 9pm or later. He was working seven days a week at that office. I still continued to be the dutiful wife and always had his dinner ready for him when he did finally walk through the door. I would try, to no avail, to engage him in conversation about his day. I would never ask him directly about work, as we would tap dance around that subject at all cost. As vague as he was about his personal life when we first met, he had become increasingly vague about his business now. I would try to tell him about my day and the dogs, etc. and could tell he just didn't want hear it or be involved in idle chit-chat. He was distracted all the time now and I was ignored on a regular basis. He was becoming completely shut off from me and began showings signs of anger when I would implore him to talk to me. I hated being so shut out.

The anger would only get worse when I would bring up Puki and her "claws" being dug deep into him and how he had changed since he began working with her. He was defensive and nasty towards me and the arguments escalated more regularly now. Dear God what happened to the smart man I fell so deeply in love with so many years ago? Where is the sweet, loving, funny man who always referred to me as his "sweetie" or his "girl"? Why can't he see how he has changed and how cruel he has become towards me and how badly he is treating me? I continued to try and be the wife I always was. But over time it was becoming very difficult for me to be kind and loving towards him and to continue to wait on him and do the things I always did for him at home while he was continuing to treat me so badly. It was around this time that I began to notice not only his "disconnection" with me physically, but also he was beginning to drink more frequently during the weeknights when he came home. This disturbed me greatly as I knew from personal experience with my own father what the beginning signs and behavior of becoming an alcoholic were. I was never more than an occasional social drinker myself and only enjoyed the occasional glass of wine or champagne among friends at gatherings.

That physical "disconnection" was unbearable. We had always had a very healthy sex life and we were always "touchy-feely" with one another. Lots of hugging, kissing, hand-holding, and cuddling. My heart was beginning to break at this point at the shear sadness of what was going on between us. I continued to fight for us and our marriage and my heart, although at odds with my brain, was not ready to give up yet. I kept telling myself that all marriages go through hard times and we would get over this hump eventually.

But then it started to get worse and the fighting was getting uglier and uglier. One evening while we were watching television, Dick was lying on the floor as he usually did after drinking several shots of vodka or tequila, or maybe both. One of the dogs was lying on his lap with the other curled up next to his side. I stood up to head upstairs and asked him if he wanted the remote control. He didn't answer so I gently dropped it next to his side to avoid hitting the dogs. As I turned away I heard him get up and he came after me and slammed me up against the wall. I was speechless to say the least and he blew up at me about throwing the remote at him and hitting his elbow. I was in shock at his explosion and totally taken off guard by it. He was not making any sense at all while he was screaming at me. I knew the alcohol only enhanced his temper and I couldn't say a word. His grip on my arm was beginning to hurt, so I screamed at him, "Go ahead and hit me, just hit me"! I really did want him to hit me. I knew the pain from it would heal a lot faster than the emotional and mental abuse he had bestowed upon me the last year. This man is almost a foot taller than me and I was terrified. He finally let me go and I ran upstairs to the bedroom and locked the doors behind me. Completely bewildered at what had just occurred, I took a pillow and blanket and closed myself up in the walk-in closet and collapsed on the floor into a fetal position shaking and crying.

We avoided each other completely for a couple of days after that incident without talking whatsoever. I would make sure I was out walking the dogs when he got up in the morning and would not come into the house until he had left for work. In the evening I would be in the bedroom with the door closed before he arrived home. He never once apologized and I began to wonder if he even remembered what he did to me that night.

Now I am not too big on going all out and celebrating a lot of holidays, but I do enjoy birthdays the most. Two weeks after the wall slam incident was my birthday. In the past Dick always made a big deal out of it and we would go out for a nice dinner in the city or join friends to celebrate. Not this year. I did not speak of my impending birthday prior to the actual day as I was hoping he would remember it without being reminded. He didn't. The entire day was filled with emails and phone calls from family and friends wishing me happy birthday, but not a peep out of him. When he finally arrived home late that night I never said a word. Of course the first thing he does upon entering the kitchen from the garage is set down his briefcase and poured himself a drink. This time it was like a triple shot and he downed it without taking a breath. We exchanged "pleasantries" and I went upstairs for a few minutes. I was so hurt! I came down stairs to find he had poured himself another drink, possibly his third already and I asked him if he knew what day it was. He mumbled and said no. I told him it was my birthday and he just looked at me and said nothing. I couldn't hold my tongue any longer.

I immediately started in on him about how he has thrown our marriage aside while he works and spends all his time with "those people" and how hurt I am. I accused him of having an affair with Puki and lying to me. I confronted him about his drinking being out of control and how he needed help. Things obviously escalated from that point and we were screaming at the tops of our lungs at each other. I realized the windows were open and just knew the neighbors would hear us yelling and call the police. It was that bad. I began to close the windows when I noticed that the two dogs were cowering together in the kitchen and I was devastated for them. I sat in the recliner and called them over to me to comfort them. One was in my lap and the other next to my feet. Dick continued to rant at me and I just ignored him. He was in the kitchen at this point and my back was to him while sitting in the recliner when all of a sudden he yelled, "Don't you dare ignore me now after what you started tonight"! Before I knew it he had picked up the recliner from the backside and dumped me and one of the dogs over onto the floor with the recliner falling on top of us. I crawled out from under the recliner and grabbed the phone and told him I would call the police if he dared touch me or came after me again. Oh my dear God who was this man? I gathered the dogs and immediately retreated to the bedroom upstairs locking the doors behind me of course. The cat had already hidden under my bed earlier when the fighting had begun. Well, happy birthday to me!

The next morning before dawn I came downstairs to find him passed out on the floor with a half glass of vodka still in his hand. I removed it so it would not spill onto the carpet and he never flinched.

The next couple of weeks we avoided each other like the plague. I think he remembered what he had done this time and neither of us knew how to deal with it. And needless to say both Rachel and Marlo upon hearing of this event and me telling them of the previous wall slam event, they both wanted me to get a restraining order against him and kick his sorry ass out immediately. I could understand their concern for me and knew they were right. But I couldn't do it. I just couldn't do it. Even after all that had happened I still loved him and felt that with time I could get back the old Dick, the man I loved so deeply. The man who loved me and treated me so sweetly. I was struggling with believing that he would throw everything away we had built together. Our marriage, our home, our family. It was like those things did not exist in his mind anymore. It was like he suddenly lost all connection to our relationship and the memories of how happy we were together.

It's Over

In November 2010 a few weeks after my birthday, my brother Tom and his lovely lady came to visit for a few days. Dick and my brother had become good friends over the years up until now. Tom knew the circumstances of what we had been going through these last couple of years and all the reasons why. No brother wants to see his sister have her heart broken. Dick went through the motions of trying to act as polite as he could during their visit. From time to time I would see the man I fell in love with come to the surface.

I never trusted what went on in that office of his. I still did not believe he was having a physical affair, but there was a connection between Dick and Puki that made the hair on the back of my neck stand up. Like I mentioned earlier, my first instinct after meeting her wasn't a good one. From time to time during an argument or even when I was just feeling quiet and sad, I would ask if he was having an affair with her and he would always deny it.

Without going into all the morbid details, and to be honest I never really knew all the details anyway, I had discovered that Dick had gotten himself into some legal issues at work. There was a great deal on his shoulders and his total focus for months had been trying to correct these work-related problems. He prided himself on always doing the right thing and being a fair businessman. Apparently he had been duped into signing some documents that she insisted he sign without even taking the time to read them and there was some kind of trouble because of it. He was actually at the point of being disbarred from practicing certain areas of the law in the state of California. Because of the apparent brainwashing of this once smart, careful businessman, she somehow had him convinced that he did not need to read everything and that he should just trust her and sign anything she asked him to. I asked myself how all this could happen. Every time I inquired about work and these new revelations he would always respond, "It's all good". He would never elaborate and I felt he was just trying to shelter me from stressing over the details of it all and also that he felt embarrassed by it all. He continued to drink heavily every night when he would arrive home in order to take his mind off work for a few hours.

For the past year we had been arguing more than ever, saying things to each other I never thought we would say to one another; terrible, hurtful things. He worked all the time now and when he was home his mind was always focused on work. It totally consumed his every waking moment. I tried to talk to him but he kept so much inside. I was feeling more and more like an outsider every day, especially in my own house. I was alone even when he was there.

We had loved each other so much before and I still thought in my heart after all we had been through lately that nothing could come between us that we couldn't overcome, until now. Those trusting instincts I inherited from my mother were dead on. If it smells like a skunk, it is a skunk!

It was late November 2010 and we were standing in the kitchen when out of the blue he told me it just wasn't working for him anymore. He said he felt we hadn't had a marriage in over a year. It felt like a knife has been stabbed straight through my heart! The pain couldn't compare to any other I had felt before. At this point we had never spoken of the marriage being in jeopardy of ending. I was still assuming that we were in a rough patch and would pull through. My knees went weak as I started to cry. "What happened to us, Dick"? He couldn't answer. He told me he would be moving out of the house soon. He was looking down at the floor and couldn't look at me. I felt like someone punched a hole in my chest. I asked him, "What am I supposed to do now"? His response was, "Get a roommate". I replied back, "I have a roommate, it's you". He did not say anything else to me. He stood there silent and staring at the floor. With something this serious and he couldn't look me in the eye.

It was that night that he moved into the spare bedroom never to sleep in our bed together again. I felt like my world had come to a screeching halt. I knew he meant it and there was no going back.

Thanksgiving that year wasn't the same obviously. It had always been my favorite holiday, but not this year. My boys and their wives came over for dinner that day. We had decided this year not to do the big turkey feast with all the trimming. Instead we prepared homemade pizzas and salads and of course pumpkin pie. It was different but oh so tasty. I loved having everyone there. Dick ate with us but didn't indulge in much conversation. He knew the kids were aware of what was going on and he was uncomfortable being around them. I knew it would be our last Thanksgiving together.

Now we have Christmas to get through. I invited Marlo and Dave over for Christmas Eve. I thought Dick might be more comfortable if it was the four of us trying to enjoy a quiet night in our home. Dick always liked Dave; they had become good drinking buddies. Why do I care about making it comfortable for him? Because I still love him. It was a bittersweet evening and after a few cocktails he kissed me on the tip of my nose and called me "his sweetie" for the last time. Part of me, my heart that is, wanted to believe he meant it and that maybe he was having a change of heart, but my mind knew better and I knew the alcohol had clouded his thoughts. That evening he went to the guest bedroom and I went to our bedroom alone.

The next day we went to the annual family Christmas dinner at Marlo and Dave's house. It was there that I asked him one more time to consider leaving the office and going back into the technology field. I mentioned us going to counseling and trying to get back to the way we were. He said he would never pay some complete stranger good money to spill his personal business to and be told by this stranger what to he needed to do. He looked me straight in the eye and said he trusted "his people" with his life and he would not leave them. Seeing as "his people" were doing some underhanded business and had gotten him involved, knowingly or unknowingly, and he was about to go to a hearing before the courts about possible disbarment in the next week or so, I asked him, "How's that working for you Dick, trusting your new family"? He just gave me a cold stare and said nothing. I was still in awe of how he could say things like that when he knew good and damn well that they were bringing him down and he was in way over his head and about to lose everything. Maybe that was it. He knew he was about to hit rock bottom and he didn't know how to get out of it and didn't want to drag me down with him. I don't know, I just don't know. As I felt before, it was like he flipped an internal switch and turned off all emotion and feelings and became this totally unrecognizable man.

New Year's Eve 2010

The sadness is overwhelming to me. The end of our love story had come. A love that I thought would last forever. But now I realized it was over for good. The distance that had grown between us was way too much to get past. The man I loved was gone forever. No amount of counseling was going to bring us back together. He had completely flipped the switch to off and I was no longer a part of anything he did or planned to do in the future. The man I loved was as cold as ice. My friends had noticed that he started treating me differently around the holidays. Before, he would dismiss me or cut me off if he didn't want to hear what I had to say. Now a mean streak had come out in him that I had never seen in the sixteen years I knew him. Our friends noticed it before I did and that's where I turned a blind eye because I loved this man so much. He was mentally abusing me and I let him do it. My friends tried, ever so gently, to tell me what I was not seeing myself at the time. But there had been such a little fighter in me who wanted to keep trying to save our marriage anyway. I didn't think I would ever be whole again. He had broken my spirit and I didn't think I would ever recover. Without an honest explanation of any kind he had ended our love story. Just like that!

Because we had already made plans well in advance, we spent our last New Year's Eve together with Marlo and Dave. It was just the four of us. I never liked big crowded venues for New Year's. We snacked on appetizers and sipped champagne and cocktails. It seemed like any other evening at their home. The only difference now was that I knew it would be our last New Year's Eve together as a couple.

Marlo and I were both in relationships that needed to be changed or removed. We were both hanging on by a thread with the men we were with. Thank goodness we had each other. Here we were, two ladies sitting in her bedroom watching televised New Year's celebrations on the east coast. Since moving to California I always celebrated New Year's on east coast time. I just couldn't stay up until midnight anymore to ring in the New Year. She and I were enjoying our girl time together. The men were downstairs drinking themselves into a stupor and not even realizing we weren't in the room with them anymore. It was 9pm when the ball dropped in New York. Marlo and I looked at each other and promised our lives would be different in 2011.

It is now February and I have gone an entire day without tears. Dick has yet to move out. There are times when I look at him and I want to wrap my arms around him and sob. My heart is breaking for him and everything he is going through. Then there are times I'm so angry I can't stand to look at him, all the while loving him still. My friends don't think he is having an affair, they think this is just his way of making me not want to be with him anymore. I know he is embarrassed, feels unworthy, his ego is shot, and he doesn't know how to act around me. I can't even wrap myself around all of this. He is still so very secretive and never speaks a word about what is going on in the office? And I never ask anymore. I look at his eyes and they are dead. Hollow. No feeling or emotion at all. How does he do that? If I am hurt, angry, sick, tired, happy or anything, it shows on my face. This is where women wear their hearts on their sleeves. The book was right, men are from Mars, and women are from Venus. This is torture.

Every day I wake up I wonder where I'll be in six months. I know I can't count on him. But I do know I can count on my friends and family if need be. All he is to me now is a "cash cow". He gives me money to pay the main expenses like utilities, car insurance, groceries, etc. He wanted it this way so this is how it is. I still think he loves me and is doing all this for my own benefit. Why does it hurt so much? One of the most painful feelings is I feel like I've lost my best friend. Any time something happened the first person I would call or get in touch with was him. We were two peas in a pod. He was Ying and I was Yang. It was a closeness some people never experience.

A Stranger in the House

March 2011. When he comes home now he doesn't even acknowledge me. I could be lying dead upstairs on the floor and he would never know. In fact that did occur one evening. I went to a movie earlier in the day and came home not feeling well. I took my pillow and blanket and went into my bedroom closet curled up in a ball on the floor and went to sleep with a bad stomach ache. Don't ask me why, but I find security and comfort in my walk in closet. When I woke up the next morning he was home. My car was in the garage and he never even came to look for me. This isn't the only time this has happened. He treats me like crap and I put up with it. I ask myself, "Why"? But I will never know the answer.

Another week of the same old stuff. Passing each other in the kitchen; he doesn't even exchange pleasantries anymore. It is so hard but at the same time I would rather he still be here. I have to learn to let go. It won't be long now.

I remember when we made our last house payment. It was in August of 2010. Those wonderful people he trusted so much had run the business into the ground and there was not much income coming into our household. This was the first time in my entire life I didn't make a rental or mortgage payment. As much as I love this house, every time I open the door I feel like a squatter; like I'm staying someplace for free. It isn't a nice feeling. My attorney and many others have said I need to let that go. There are many people in the same situation as I am. Rachel had lost her great job of eleven years in 2008 and was in the same boat. She too had purchased her dream home in 2004 and was now losing her home to an impending foreclosure. She was lucky and found another job that same year, but took a huge cut in salary. There was no saving her house. I know there are many other people in this country right now facing the same heartbreak as I am, but right now I don't care about the others. I only care about us! This is what he does now for a living by the way. Helping people save their homes with loan modifications. Between his legal and real estate licenses this was the career direction he took. Why didn't he try to save ours? Knowing we could have done something to try and keep the house still rattles me. He had known all along for quite some time that he didn't want to stay in the house and wanted no part of it or me any longer. So many signs - the light bulb just never went off. I think he has been trying to leave me for two years; he just wasn't man enough. I would ask him, "Is everything alright"? His answer to everything was always, "It's all good". The communication ceased between us the minute Puki and her people entered into our lives. He was under her spell.

I knew we would be losing our dream home and then where was I supposed to live when that happened? He still says he is moving out and it will be within the next month. He says he will continue to give me money every month to pay the minimum household expenses and nothing more. With what he was giving me and my small income from social security, I was barely getting by. How on earth was I going to afford rent for an apartment once I was out on my own? My car is paid for free and clear but I still have insurance and maintenance on it. I only have one credit card in my name and it was maxed out thanks to Dick asking me to get a large cash advance from it to help during the time he had minimal income coming in from the business. But I also have monthly pet expenses and pretty soon I will have to begin paying for Medicare. I had obtained an attorney but was in no hurry to file for divorce. The expense of that process was something I didn't have the means to cover at this time, much less the emotional capacity to deal with right away.

I had started to entertain the idea of moving back to the east coast to be closer to my family. When I shared this thought with Dick he immediately thought it was what I should do. Little did I know at the time that he had ulterior motives for wanting to get me out of our house as soon as possible.

He told me when I vacated the house that I should rent it to a friend who was considering moving to the bay area. He said to rent it for $1,800 a month and I could have $900 and he could have $900. I asked him if that was illegal to take money from someone and keeping it when we haven't made a mortgage payment in six months. He said it was fine as long as the house wasn't in foreclosure proceedings yet. He said if I didn't rent it to my friend when I moved out that he was going to rent it to someone else. I asked how he thought he would be entering the house since I planned to change the locks as soon as he moved out. He simply said, "Break the locks". He has an answer for everything. I don't trust a word that comes out of his mouth. I would rather burn the house to the ground before I let him rent it to strangers. Especially when we could have re-financed the house two years ago together to reduce the payments. His ethics have turned to shit!

Some days are better than others. Every now and again I can see the man I fell in love with start to peek through. It might only last for a minute, then as quickly as it appears it fades away. If I had to pick a roommate he would be the perfect one. He hardly speaks, surprisingly makes his bed, picks up after himself, and is only home maybe a total of 2-3 hours a day, other than to sleep. He has completely shut himself off from me in every way, shape and form. It's 7pm on a Saturday night. Where is he? I'm not allowed to ask. I still consider myself his wife, but he apparently doesn't see me that way. Out of respect or common courtesy he could at least pick up the phone and say he would be home in an hour. Whatever! Why do I even care? In the past he would text "in car". That meant he was on his way home. I wish I could find that switch he flipped. I would switch it to off just to end my pain. I hate it when he calls me by name now. He had always called me his "sweetie" and now that is gone. I swear those people he works with, the ones he trusts with his life, are turning him against us more and more every day. When he opens his mouth I hear someone else's verbiage. It's Puki's. This highly educated and intelligent man is falling further into the dumps with every day he spends around that office.

I am getting ready to visit family and my BFF Rachel in Florida. It will be a nice break from what I have been living with these past months. Being with family is just what the doctor ordered. It will be the best therapy I could have asked for. Again, family will be there to get me through my sadness and tears. I need to hug my grandchildren, my son, my Rachel.

Getting ready to head back to California. This has been an amazing trip for me and although I feel broken down on the inside, I was able to enjoy being with the kids. Rachel and I got the opportunity to have dinner at our favorite seafood restaurant on the bay at sunset. My silly girl had framed two 8 x 10 color photos to accompany us on our dinner date. Mine was of Carlisle Cullen and hers was Edward Cullen. Our Twilight loves! We sat them on the table with us at the restaurant and didn't care what other people thought of us. We shared a bottle of champagne and split a dinner of crab cakes and salad and laughed until we cried. The waiter did not share our enthusiasm when we asked him to take a photo of us with our dates. After dinner we went to a very famous restaurant that we had frequented many times in the past for dessert and coffee.

This is the first time I didn't want to go home except to see to see my pets and friends. I'll walk into what was once a home filled with love and joy into a house that is just that, a house. The love that once filled the inside is gone. I don't know what to expect from him when I arrive. I do know that he was home every night at a decent time while I was out of town. Unlike when I'm there and he arrives after 9 pm every night. This is how it's been for the past year and I wasn't supposed to get upset. If I wanted to be a party of one I would have remained single!

Not sure how long he plans to stay living with me as a roommate. I sometimes wish he would leave but there is a piece of my heart that wants him to stay. This is the hard part, knowing once he leaves the locks get changed and he is dead to me. At least that is what I am trying to convince myself of. This is the only way I can deal with this for now; to totally cut off all communication and try to adjust to him being completely out of my life. Time will tell when I'm ready to call or text him. There won't be any of, "Can I come over and see the dogs" or "I left something in the garage and need to pick it up". I have to be the one to put the wall up for now. I'm not good at closing myself off from things, especially the man I thought I would spend the rest of my life with. I want to hug him and slap him at the same time. God help me this is more difficult than I ever imagined!

I think I'll miss the touch of his hand on mine as we are in the car and he would reach over and give me a gentle tap or the kiss on the forehead at night or sitting in a movie and feeling his shoulder next to mine. Not to mention the intimacy of being a married couple. I liked being married but not the way it is now.

Pets Are Family and Friends Too!

This part of the book seems to be the most difficult to write. Where to start? Everyone that owns a pet will relate to this chapter. There is nothing like walking through the front door and no matter what your day was like someone was glad to see you. That someone is your pet. I think pets in general might be smarter than people at times. Unconditional love is what they give us no matter what. They are totally dependent on us for everything. It is almost like bringing a new child into the home. You can tell them anything and they will sit there and listen like they understand every word you speak. The comfort and joy they give us goes a long way. Have you ever noticed how many homeless people keep their pets with them? It's the feeling of their warmth against you when you are sitting in a chair reading or watching television that makes you all warm and fuzzy inside. Then there are times when you ask yourself, "What was I thinking bringing a pet into the house"? I have never vacuumed so much in my life as I do having two Pugs and a Persian cat! Do we realize what we spend on them? Cheap is not a word you can use in the same sentence when talking about your pets. Food, toys, clothes, visits to the vet, boarding and grooming. Who can afford a vacation after you pay for the boarding? There is nothing left! Do we care really? Not in my house! They are family and the comfort they bring is what gets me through the rough days. They lick away my tears and seem to understand that mommy's heart is broken.

I've had pets my entire life, mostly cats. I have previously had five dogs prior to getting our two Pugs. All five of these dogs, big and small, none of them cost me what these Pugs cost. Never once did I have to pay for an "anal gland extraction"! OMG... doesn't that sound ugly? And it has an even nastier odor! But truly, how can you put a price on the joy and comfort your pets bring to you?

I've only had to put one pet to sleep; it was one of the hardest things I've ever had to do. It was my Persian cat, Mr. Honey. He was with me for twelve wonderful years when he started losing weight and not eating. I knew it was inevitable; his time was soon coming to an end. The vet said he had cancer throughout his little body and to bring him home and make him as comfortable as possible. He would let me know when he was ready. We had him another four days when one morning when it was time to feed him, he looked up at me and just fell over on his side.

I called the vet and they said to bring him in. Dick was in classes at law school when I called him and he came home so we could do this together.

We were only a few miles from the vet hospital and the drive seemed so very long. I had him in an orange towel petting him, singing to him, and just loving him his last few hours with us. When we arrived we were immediately taken to a private room. Everyone was so kind and caring, knowing what was about to happen. His little body felt and looked so frail. Working at an animal hospital would be way too hard for me; I am too emotional. But the staff here was amazing. I don't know how they do it. We were there a few minutes when our vet came in and told us what he would be doing to Mr. Honey. He would take him into another room and insert an IV in his little paw and then bring him back and we could then say our good-byes. I had only seen Dick cry once before and when I looked up at that very moment, tears were streaming down his face. He was sobbing like a little boy. I was shocked at his emotions and I didn't know how to comfort him. Hell, I couldn't comfort myself! I was just glad we could be there together when this little family friend that we loved so much would take his last breath. The injection was administered as I cradled him in my arms. It was like he just went to sleep. I knew he was ready and I know he knew how loved he was. My heart aches as I write this. It was one of the saddest things I've ever experienced. If you are a pet owner I know you understand.

The drive home was painful for both of us. I felt even closer to him than I had before. We didn't talk, but just held hands as he drove quietly back to our apartment in the city. When we got home we just held each other and cried.

I know the day will come when my dogs and cat will pass on to pet heaven and I will cherish all the unconditional love and strength they have given me over the years. I truly believe my pets know how much they are loved. They have literally lifted me out of depression and dark times. Too many times to count.

Trying to Take Charge of my Life

I've been in bed all day with a mild case of the flu. He comes home again at 9pm. I fix his dinner like a dummy and then go back to bed. Do you think he could even ask me how I'm feeling? Why do I put up with him? I am being treated like a stranger in my own home. Who knows? I certainly don't and I am too tired of trying to figure it out anymore.

Two full days of crying my eyes out and staying in the house. I can't stand to be around people. I hate "acting" like I am happy when I am not. I take my walk every morning; walk the dogs and go to dance class... that's it! Walking into the grocery store makes me anxious. I can't put it off any longer. I am going to my doctor to get anxiety meds. I need something to help me not want to jump out of my skin. The doctor visit was a success! I have a prescription for an anti-anxiety pill that just takes the edge off when the nerves start creeping in and getting a hold of me. So far, so good. At least I have something that works and hopefully it will at least help me to sleep at night so I can shut my mind off. Night time is the worst of course; lying in bed alone with my mind running rampant.

Time is getting closer for him to move out of the house. He told me the other night he would be leaving in a couple of weeks. To be honest, it can't come soon enough and he knows when he leaves that's it. After everything he has put me through and for my own peace of mind, I have to treat it like he has died. Because literally, the wonderful man I fell in love with has indeed died. It is the only way I can deal with it right now. We have lived with his terms for the past sixteen years and now it will be on my terms how I want to handle this. They say time heals all wounds. I'll believe that when it happens. Right now it feels like I won't ever recover from the pain, hurt, heartache or mistrust I am feeling. I am scared thinking about the upcoming move and starting a new life at my age. Twenty years ago I did it without blinking an eye, but this is a different time we live in now.

Just when I thought there were no jobs to be had, I was offered a part time position close to home three days a week with decent pay. It couldn't have come at a better time. Just when one door closes another one opens.

March 13th, my lucky number is 13. Today I am finally going to take charge and stop whining and feeling sorry for myself. Yes, I am devastated, heartbroken, blindsided, afraid, scared, broke and sad. So very, very sad. Someone asked me if I felt ashamed. Why the hell should I be ashamed? I kept my vows. I loved and supported unconditionally the man who I thought I would spend the rest of my life with, even though I didn't get the same in return. My head hung low for awhile because I was so sad. I didn't want to have eye contact with anyone or anything. Now I hold my head up high and know that I did everything possible I could to save our marriage. The one thing I am definitely NOT is alone. I have the most wonderful family and support system that give me strength and guidance every day. Their love has made me a better and much stronger person. I know that it is time for me to take charge of ME. For the past sixteen years I was taking care of someone else.

His Departure

April 2011. If he'd had his way he would have stayed in the house living in the spare bedroom indefinitely; it didn't seem to bother him in the least. We had spoken on several occasions as to the actual move-out date and yet he continued to prolong it. He wasn't concerned the mortgage was not being paid; he had all the luxuries without the expense. Including a live-in housekeeper, cook, and caregiver named Carlie. Yeah, that's me! I finally had enough and one evening I confronted him and said, "This isn't working for me any longer". "I can't heal and begin to move on with my life with you living here like a roommate under the same roof". "You have to leave". And with no emotion at all, he simply replied, "I will be out this coming weekend".

He is on his way home and it's only 6:30pm, this is a first in months! We are going to our favorite Mexican restaurant one last time together. This is a safe place to have conversation and not get into any kind of confrontation. I have a few things I want to tell him before he moves out tomorrow and will try to keep it light in order to avoid an argument or make him hostile. I want him to know how I feel and how sorry I am this had happened to us. I want him to remember the wonderful, fun, sweet, spontaneous adventures we had together and everything else that defined the love we shared. It was the most special, safe love I've ever felt. My heart needed to tell him this.

My friends say I will be much better once he leaves the house. The anticipation of him coming home every night and knowing he is just across the hall sleeping is too hard for me to bear and I cannot heal as long as he is still here. When he is around me he does everything he can avoid looking at me or talking to me. I initiated any and all conversation we had. The days of us laughing and calling each other our little pet names was over. It's sad when a relationship ends especially when both parties still love each other. No one ever prepares oneself for this to happen when you think you've finally married your life partner. Oh well, life goes. Right? They say we are never given more than we can handle. For the time being I have handled as much as I can regarding this marriage.

It's Sunday and today's the day. My heart is heavy and I feel like there is a fog around me that I'm trying desperately to find my way out of. Marlo came over early this morning to be with me while he moved. I didn't want to be alone and her support and just being there by my side distracting me was just what I needed. By the time she had arrived he had already left to meet the cable people at his new apartment. At this point he had not shared with me exactly where he was moving to. He came back to the house, backed his car into the garage and started putting his clothes in the trunk. Meanwhile, I stayed out in the backyard with Marlo and the dogs. I went in the house just in time to find him standing in the garage crying. We sobbed in each other's arms holding each other tightly. I have never cried so many tears in my life. I had bagged up some of the groceries from the pantry that were items only he would eat and he had noticed I put them in the backseat of his car. I had slipped a framed photo from our wedding day and another photo of us from a memorable vacation into the bag as well. I am not sure why I put those pictures in that bag for him. I guess I just wanted him to have something to remind him of the happier times we shared together. I sat in my favorite chair after he left, stroking the dogs and cat until late that evening. Marlo had stayed and I guess we watched chick flicks all day; I can't remember, I was too numb. I slept on the family room sofa that night, and many nights to follow. He hadn't slept with me since November and this is now mid-April. I just couldn't face being upstairs knowing he was now gone for good. Even during the time he slept in a room across the hall from me, I at least didn't feel completely alone.

The most difficult thing for me that day was opening the closet doors and his clothes were all gone. If I didn't know before, I knew then he was never coming back. The emptiness I felt was overwhelming.

It wasn't until three days later when I went to get something from the garage that I noticed he had left the wedding picture behind on the shelf. The pain in my chest was unbearable and had me crying on the garage floor holding our picture wondering how did this happen. After sixteen years he leaves, never really explaining why, and now I have to pick up the pieces all alone.

Almost a week has passed and we haven't talked, emailed or texted one another. This is how I need it to be for now. I have to mourn what has happened in my life like someone died. So many times I wanted to send a text message asking how he was. Staying strong is hard for me. My heart wants to reach out to him but my mind is telling me not to. I guess since I have not heard from him that for once he actually listened to me and took me literally when I said that after he moved out he would be dead to me. I didn't realize how alone I felt until the following weekend arrived. He was now gone and my three boys, their wives, and my grandchildren were all on the east coast to attend a family wedding. My grandchildren are in the wedding and my son is sending me pictures and updates throughout the festivities all weekend in hopes that I would not feel left out and so alone. I didn't realize how much I missed everyone. I hope I don't feel like this after leaving the west coast. Oh the sadness!

Dick's son Wade is flying in from the east coast tonight; he is on spring break from college. He wants to stay at the house with me for most of his visit. I am so looking forward to our time together. It will be good to cook a meal for someone again. A "party of one" meal lately for me has been cereal, fruit, soup or salads. My grocery bill will be less now, that's for sure. I have to look at anything that is positive and saving money is the most positive thing I am focusing on right now.

Dick was picking Wade up from the airport close to midnight and was dropping him off at the house. How strange is that? Dick's own son wanting to stay with me instead of his own father. And how awkward I felt for his son just being dropped off like a package left at the front door. Wade had texted me when he was just minutes from the house so I turned on the porch light and peeked out the front window looking for him to arrive. Dick's car pulled in front of the house and as Wade unloaded his suitcase I opened the front door, all the while standing behind it. Dick pulled away quickly before Wade reached the front door. It is nice having Wade in the house again. I haven't seen him in almost a year. I can now talk to someone other than the dogs; not that they aren't good listeners, however a little adult conversation is also nice. Besides, the dogs couldn't carry their end of the conversation very well anyway. Within the first hour of Wade being with me I found the courage to ask him how he thought his father was. He replied "embarrassed", I made no comment. Our visit has been very stress free and relaxing. I think when Dick was at home and his boys would come to visit there was more tension between all of us for some reason. Two weeks and this is the longest Dick and I have ever gone without some kind of contact. I knew he was moving somewhere close to his office and knowing he was only twenty minutes away wasn't easy. I am constantly in fear that I may run into him and I have too many mixed emotions right now to deal with that.

Wade and I had a wonderful time together and after a couple of days I felt comfortable sharing some of the "history" of the demise of the marriage to his father. Not the truly ugly parts, but mostly the sad parts and how heartbroken I was. One evening as I was crying while sharing some of my heartache with him about what his father and I had been going through, Wade thought it would be a good idea to take down and remove all the pictures in the house of his father and I together in happier times. He felt like these pictures were just painful reminders for me and he was right. What a wise, young man.

Wade stayed with me for four nights and during that entire time he never once heard from his father. He left on a Wednesday morning and stayed with his father for only two nights. Coming home to a quiet, empty house takes some getting used to. I like it and I don't, if that makes any sense. I'm not crying as much as I have been; I'm living through a different emotion every hour it seems.

Easter weekend and my two sons and their lovely wives came over for a cookout. The kids prepared the entire meal. I love that all three of my sons like to cook as does my brother and myself! I guess it runs in the family. It was a lovely visit and we always laugh a lot when we are all together. I know my boys knew that I was raw with heartache and the conversations that afternoon and evening veered away from anything having to do with "him". After I closed the door bidding farewell that sinking loneliness rushed back in with a vengeance. The house seems so big and empty when I'm by myself. Thank God I have the pets; they are keeping me sane.

Keeping myself busy has helped more than I could have imagined. Between my part time job, dance classes, keeping up the yard, the house, and three pets, my days are pretty full. Week four since he left, and still not a word. It is time for me to receive my first check from him to cover the monthly household expenses, etc. He had promised when he moved out that he would continue to provide the funds to cover these expenses, excluding the mortgage payment of course. I have sent two very polite text messages to him over the last several days regarding a months' worth of mail for him that had accumulated at the house and reminding him that I needed the money soon to pay bills. No response whatsoever! The third message isn't going to be as civil. He is still screwing with my mind; he has been for the past sixteen years. Well, what do you know... three days after the second text and he finally responded that he had received my messages and would come by later that day to pick up his mail and give me a check. I was in the house when he arrived but had set his mail outside by the front door. He left the check in the mailbox and that was it. I didn't need to speak to him nor did I want to see him; I just wanted my money.

Living Alone

This is the second time in my life I've lived all by myself. I had a parent, grandparent, husband or children living with me at any given time throughout my life. When I relocated to San Francisco in June of 1994 I moved into a sweet one bedroom Victorian apartment, within walking distance to everything and anything. It was just what I dreamed living in San Francisco would be like. The apartment had high ceilings with all this magnificent detail; the living room had three huge bay windows and it was located right on the corner. I could see up and down the streets in all four directions. My kitchen had a window seat facing out through three bay windows and you could see my dishes through the vintage, glass enclosed cabinets in the kitchen. The bathroom was small with a window and my small bedroom had a wall of closets and three more bay windows with a fire escape I could sit out on and enjoy the street traffic. I loved it! I loved coming home on the bus every night from work and walking through four sets of doors to my little haven called home. July 1994 until May 1995 it was just me and my cat, Mr. Honey. It was the happiest I had felt in a very long time. I only had myself to answer to and I loved every single minute of it. Every day I enjoyed my own company. This was something I never had the chance or time to do in my life before and I loved the independence and not having to take care of anyone else but myself and my cat!

In hindsight, some place deep inside me resented him for coming into my world at this time. However, I was so happy when we were together and it didn't seem to matter. He started moving in a little at a time the following May, 1995. We eventually had to move into a larger place and found this wonderful one bedroom flat in the Avenues; one of the many areas you would be privileged to live in San Francisco. It was another place we called home; it had everything that you would expect living in the city. This is where we really fell in love. I remember waking up one night and he was caressing my neck and gently said I love you. I knew he loved me by his actions and just the way he was when we were together. It was the first time he ever said the words out loud.

The flat was my favorite place we lived in the city. It was too bad we were only there for a little over a year when he was offered an opportunity to move back to the east coast with his company. I was happy just being with him. He was my best friend, confidant, lover, and he was my other half.

So This is How it's Going to be

It has been almost a month since he moved out of the house. I sent an email letting him know he had mail. No response from him whatsoever. I guess I really didn't expect one. I then sent a text message asking if I could have my money for May before the weekend. I always end my text messages with a "thank you." Again no response; did I expect anything else? I gave him until the next day, twenty four hours to be exact, requesting he show me some respect and answer my text messages. I had bills to pay. Just because he doesn't pay his, that's not how I work. He finally answered and stated he was stopping by at 4:30 the following day to collect his mail. In the meantime, I came home from work on Thursday and my check for May was in the mailbox. It was only half of what I was supposed to get; he had already cut me back last month by $500 and now it was even less. At first I thought maybe he was going to send in two payments and that would be fine with me.

At 4:30 on the dot I heard a knock at the door and of course the dogs started to bark. I let him in, but he didn't move far from the door. I had his mail ready for him in a plastic bag and then asked about the money. He said that was it for the month! I was at such disbelief I didn't know how to react. I felt like I had been punched in the stomach all over again. I asked him how I was supposed to pay bills and survive on this. He coldly blurted out that if his business goes under I'll get nothing. I felt my blood pressure starting to rise. My immediate comeback to him was, "Get another job! You pay your employees so why is it so difficult to pay me"? He then so bitterly answered, "I don't pay them as much as I pay you"! I couldn't believe what I was hearing; I took care of this man for sixteen fucking years. I waited on him hand and foot, folded his underwear the way he wanted, hung his shirts the way he requested, bought all his favorite snacks, kept his house immaculate, took care of all the maintenance on our vehicles, paid the bills and by God gave him the best sex of his life! I could go on and on. That he had the nerve to say that and speak to me that way only made his true colors shine through. That's when I said, "I'll let my attorney take care of this". Before he picked up his mail I stared him straight in his eyes and said, "Tell that whore you work with to go in the safe and get some cash". The look he shot me made the hair on the back of my neck stand up. I don't think he realized that I knew they kept a large amount of cash in the office. A few minutes later I sent a text saying, "See you in court"! First thing I did was call my girlfriend for comfort; she is always there for me.

Thursday night is my dance class and all I could think was, How am I going to get through it? Our show is only a month away and now is not a good time to miss a class. I came home, showered, never ate, and sat in my chair with the dogs. As they lay sleeping on my lap I kept wondering, "How did it get to this? I poured a glass of wine and called it a night.

Friday was much better. I usually don't work on Fridays, but there is a big event we are hosting next week and there was still plenty to do. It was good to be working; it kept my mind off things. I made an appointment to see my attorney on Tuesday. I'll feel better after we talk.

It's my first Mother's Day without him in sixteen years… guess I better get used to it. My family and friends all called to wish me a happy day. I woke up sick that morning with a stomach flu that lasted two days, so I was pretty much out of it for the day. My son and daughter-in-law came over and spent a few hours with me. It was all I could do to muster the strength to talk. Spending as much time as possible with the boys is so precious to me right now; especially with the move coming in a few months. No matter how bad I felt, it was good to see them both; it brought me a few hours of comfort. I don't know if it's because it's Mother's Day and I'm sick and alone in this big house, but the kids just left and the tears are pouring out of my eyes again. I have such a sadness looming over me right now. I hate all these emotions... are things ever going to be normal again? What the hell is normal anyway?

I went to see my attorney today after work. When Dick decided on his own to cut my money in half for the month with no warning, I needed to find out what my legal options were. Every day this man I loved for so many years surprised me more and more with his lack of emotion and feeling. Just when I thought he couldn't or wouldn't hurt me anymore, he would throw anther curveball at me.

My Thursday night dance class with the ladies will be coming to an end soon. It's bittersweet leaving this year. I've danced with these ladies since 2005; it was just what the doctor ordered. I knew I had to take a break from dancing for a year; my knees needed a rest. If I wasn't leaving I still wouldn't have danced next year. My body aches; it is telling me it needs a timeout. This isn't to say I won't dance again; I'm just going to take a little break. Next year I will be in the audience smiling and knowing all the hard work that goes into the show each year. There is an angel named Ms. D and we are all lucky she is a part of our lives.

Six more weeks until our show; I love the stage now as much as I did all those years ago. Once I get under the lights and hear the music and feel the energy and cheering from the audience, it's hard to get me to exit the stage! I love seeing all the little dancers, gaining their confidence and security from what they have learned all year. It's proud for a parent to come see your child perform no matter what their talent.

It's been almost two weeks since Dick and I spoke. I had to send an email requesting tax and medical documents and so far have received nothing. It's different when he needs something; the world stops and takes care of him. I've jumped through his hoop for the last time. He can go shit in his hat!

Father of the Year

The latest of Dick wanting to redeem himself is to become "Father of the Year". His oldest son attends college back east. It is a very hard school to get into and even more difficult to complete. The younger son just turned nineteen, graduating in May from high school. The only job he has ever held was doing yard work and now he is working with one of his mom's friends. It might not be his dream job, but at least he is working; nowadays that's almost a rarity with our poor economy. He has no idea what he wants to do with his life. His brother knew since he was in the seventh grade what he wanted to pursue in the way of a career.

Dick attends his youngest son James' graduation ceremony and puts the idea in his head to leave his home, friends, and family to move to California and work for him in his office. He just can't stand the idea that his son doesn't have a goal in life yet. Not many kids know what they want to do as far as a career at nineteen years old. Believe me; he is much safer living at home with his mom working in the Midwest than with his dad at the present time and that evil woman.

After returning from graduation Dick called James and tells him he has a job for him being a roadie with a "rock star" on a summer European tour. Dick's son would be gone for the entire summer. James is a naïve, impressionable young man who has never been away from home for more than a week. The only time James ever traveled were band trips or Boy Scout camps, and visiting his dad and me in California.

Any other time I would have been all for it. Now wasn't the time. My soon to be ex isn't in a good place mentally or financially. I truly believe he is making promises he cannot keep. He just wants to try and control his young son's life the way he thinks it should be lived. Dick is in fear that his son may waste valuable time while trying to "find himself" and figure out what he wants to do with his life. Since when did Dick have any associations with a "rock star"?

My stepson's mother and I tried to talk him out of coming to California, but he wanted to come and see for himself what his father was selling him.

His father tells his son "it's all good"; that's his comeback for everything! It's so far from "all good". I'm so afraid those people in the office will brainwash James just like they did his father. I think the "rock star" ploy was just to get him pumped up and wanting to come here for some grand adventure. I know Dick; he thinks once James is here he will stay. I pray that doesn't happen, not now. I don't put it past Dick to try to move his young, impressionable son away from his mother. Dick needs a "control" fix and seems to think his son is his best bet.

So James arrives in California. During his stay with his father, a woman from the office, a complete stranger, took my nineteen year old stepson clothes shopping. I found that a little strange, but like I've mentioned before, everything has been strange since Dick started working there. I won't even go into the style of clothes they bought him.

James arrived at the house to spend time with me on a Friday. It was good to see him. I could tell he was happy to be out of the office and away from the "harem" that follows Dick around on a daily basis. James would tell me about the "girls" bringing him food every two hours, buttering his bagel, giving him cokes all day long, not to mention the clothes shopping expedition! He said his favorite time of the day was going to the restroom so he could get away from the computer and all the unwanted attention. It was making him extremely uncomfortable. He was being smothered with attention and I don't think this was the job for him. I am glad he came out and saw for himself how things really are and it gave him a clearer perspective of the whole situation. When a marriage ends it is always sad. When there are kids involved it is even worse. Now there are other hearts to factor into place. It didn't take James long to realize that the whole "rock star" roadie job was in fact just a ruse made up by his father to lure him out to the West Coast.

I watched both my stepsons grow up from little boys to fine young men. The oldest was closer to his dad and the youngest was closer to his mom. The boys and I became closer once they entered high school. I didn't treat them as little boys anymore, they were young men. I always thought their dad was hard on them, but he was the boss when they came to our house. He just somehow felt the need to boost his testosterone by being almost mean and too strict with them. When the boys were smaller he would go to the Midwest to visit them. They would stay at a hotel with an indoor pool and it was a boy's weekend of junk food, staying up late watching movies and swimming. As they got older they would come to California to visit us. I don't think there is one place in the Bay area they didn't visit. The last couple of years they would come visit separately; it seemed to work out better that way for everyone. Individually their father could give each one of the boys his undivided attention.

Once he started working with her, the boys' visits were far and few between. He was just too busy, even for his own kids. That tells you something! Even the boys took a back seat to their father's job and her, just like me.

I enjoyed my visits with both my stepsons; there was an element of comfort having them here. Just because their dad and I are no longer together doesn't mean I won't still be a part of their lives. Once I'm living back in the DC area they can come visit all the history in our Nation's Capital and stay at the cottage on the Bay, jet ski, fish, swim; whatever they can find to do.

It was a lonely week after James flew back home. I mentioned earlier how nice it is to have another human being in the house to talk to. We had a great visit. There aren't too many nineteen year olds that would sit and watch the Twilight movies with their stepmom.

Their mom did a great job bringing these two young men up as a single mother. I know what a difficult task that can be. I am proud to be their step-mom.

Learning to do Things on my Own

I need help with my computer. He always fixed these technical things. I tried to fix it and made it worse. It's the little things like this that lures back the anger within me. I am trying my best to "adjust" and "accept" and move on with my life. These instances only remind me of how dependent I was on him as my husband to handle such things. I am so mad at him I could scream. This is where I show my weakness; there are some things I just can't do, and I'm not ashamed to admit it.

It's now June 2011. Two months since he left. I'm still having computer problems and had to break down and finally call him a couple of times to help me. What else was I supposed to do? He set up my computer and had fixed it before. Besides, it wasn't like I had the money to take it to a computer store tech for repair. It is still so hard for me to hear his voice. It sounds like the man I once loved so much, however, the verbiage is not the same. I have to remember this isn't the man I fell in love with. I ache to have that man back, but I know that is never going to happen. I can go for days not shedding a single tear, then out of nowhere something comes over me and it starts all over again. It happened just yesterday; I was fine one moment and the next I was a mess.

I cried myself to sleep again last night. Is this ever going to end? My heart has such a big hole in it and it feels like it will never heal.

The reality of the move is starting to sink in. As I walk from room to room I am making a mental list of things that will move back to the east coast with me. Hopefully a lot of the things I'm leaving behind will sell in the yard sale; I really need the money for the move expenses. I am so proud of myself; I was never much good at saving money. I have put aside every paycheck from my part time job plus any money from items of furniture I've sold. The yard sale will be a big help. There are no credit cards I can use for the move since he stopped paying them. I had a credit card of my own and it is gone also because of the financial situation he got us into. I know everything will work out; I will make sure of that! I have no choice.

My computer broke again and my son came over this time to fix it so I could continue writing my book. I asked Dick nicely if he could bring me a new computer since he has several extras sitting in the office because they had to let a few people go. He eventually drops the computer tower at my door unbeknownst to me and leaves it there. This man has three degrees in computer science and he knows I am not tech savvy. Guess it's time to learn. If I had been one of his "people" from the office he would sure as hell have fixed their computer and got it running for them right away.

I know I had said that once he moved out he would be dead to me, and I meant it. But that was just my terms until I was ready and felt strong enough to deal with him again without feeling too stressed or emotional.

I know we aren't living together anymore, but I had hoped he would still give me some help if I needed it. It wasn't like I was asking him to move furniture or paint a room. I just needed my computer to work for me and he knew how frustrated I got when it came to electronics and he always knew just what to do. The feelings of abandonment were never stronger than at this very moment. It was clear that he felt I wasn't his responsibility any longer. He acted "inconvenienced" now.

This is where friends and family come to the rescue. I asked my son to try and help me set up the new computer. I had a problem and I asked for help and received it! I didn't need his stupid computer tower after all. Between my son and a good friend, I am up and running. He can take his computer back and shove it up his ass.

It is now a little over a week until my show. After breaking two small toes on my right foot three weeks ago I think I'll be able to do it. It was a clumsy move on my part. This will be my first show in six years that Dick hasn't attended.

He would always give me a big bouquet of flowers after the show. Part of me is hoping he will come after the curtain goes up and watch my numbers, then leave before I know he was there. Every year after the show we go to our favorite Mexican restaurant for an after party with our friends and family. He is always the host, making sure everyone is taken care of, ordering the margaritas and food, boasting about his "sweetie". Not this year. It makes me so sad.

It's not that I can't do things on my own with effort and a little patience; it's just that he did certain things when we were together. The things that made him feel "manly" and needed. I can do whatever I set my mind to, although still nothing computer-related. It's not a big deal; I'm adapting to being a party of one. As anyone who has been through it before knows, it is not easy.

It's Thursday night, off to my last dance class at the studio before rehearsals start on stage.

It's Father's Day, first time in sixteen years we haven't been together or in touch with one another. I sent him a Happy Father's Day text. I would do the same for anyone. It is another beautiful day in the Bay area; I think I'll go outside and take in the sunshine with the dogs

I didn't cry all day; baby steps.

What Happened?

Webster's Dictionary: Tear: a drop of salty liquid that comes out of your eye when you are crying.

I've cried so much the skin under my eyes is raw from my salty tears. Another night of loneliness. It's all about him; always was, now, past and future. Right now life really sucks.

Before Dick moved out I recall asking him questions, just to get some kind of a response from this man. One evening I remember letting out my emotions. But as usual, no response whatsoever from him. He had turned to stone. I had asked him if it bothered him that I was being forced to move 3,000 miles away. Away from my sons, family and friends, but most of all, away from the city and area I loved the most. His response, "Do what you need to do". Not what I wanted to hear. I deserved so much better. God how I wish I didn't still love him so much. Well, the man he used to be that is.

Because my financial situation won't allow me to stay in California, my brother is buying us a place on the east coast to share. I will pack my belongings, sell what I don't need, and move to my home state. It saddens me to leave behind my children, friends, activities, weather and so much more. I love living in California. I thought this is where I would take my last breath.

I'm not a bitch. However, I can become one in a heartbeat if I'm pushed far enough. Asking for certain things when a spouse leaves is a hard thing to do. Who gets the couch? Who gets the dishes? Who gets this and who gets that? It goes on and on. Why do people get married? Every time I go to a wedding I am sad, knowing it is only going to last for maybe ten years if they're lucky. It's just a piece of paper for crying out loud! If you don't legalize then you don't have to finalize! I'm starting to sound bitter.

Any time a marriage ends it is devastating to those involved. It's like there is a death in the family. You have to go through all the emotions; grief, anger, sadness, loneliness, emptiness. You question, "Where am I going" and "What am I going to do"? Who will be there for me? The hard part is when one of the two parties in the relationship still wants to save the marriage and the other doesn't. It's just heartbreaking.

For me the most difficult piece of the puzzle was when he was still in living in our home, sleeping with the door closed to the spare bedroom. I remember every night when the door would shut I felt like there was a knife entering my heart. I tried not to cry but the tears came anyway. Who do I call when I feel like this? My BFF Rachel, that's who. She listens while I sob and repeat the same things over and over again. Never once complaining. Instead she comforts me and say's things that make me think this isn't the end of my world.

Some days are better than others, I just read the book "The Secret". It was a wonderful, uplifting read. So many things I am now experiencing were in the pages of this book. I felt as I was reading that the book had been written specifically for me at this time in my life.

All the pictures of the two of us have been taken down and packed away. Why look at the way it was, it will never be that way again. He made his choice to end things and make a new life with his new work family. There are too many of them to fight. I feel like the past three years I have been in battle with them and I finally have to concede. I've been given no choice in the matter.

This ordeal has been exhausting! I have put up with it and fought over it way too long. My husband went over to the other side, the dark side, and I don't see him coming back. To be honest, I don't want him back. Not this stranger. I don't know or care to know him. The man I married is gone forever. We had something so special, it can't even be explained. He is a completely different person than I married. I still love him but I don't like him anymore… so very sad.

Signing up for Medicare

Does the whole world know when a person is turning 65! I get mail every day from someone wanting me to go with their Medicare plans. Talk about confusing. There is so much information it is overwhelming. I always had my health insurance through my work, so all the decisions were already in place. There were minimal choices and it was easy. It still blows my mind that I'm turning 65. I still think of myself as 50!

Remember when 65 seemed ancient? I used to believe after a person turned 40 they needed to take another driving test. I soon changed my mind when I got to be that age. Then 50 came and went... those ten years sped by.

It is an overwhelming task reading the pages of information being sent to me by so many Medicare carriers. I think I finally found what hopefully will work for me, so the time has come to make the call and enroll. I don't feel 65 and I certainly don't think I look, dress, think or act 65!

A very nice gentleman from my insurance of choice came to the house and sat down explaining my options for Medicare. I finally signed up. Come September 1st, 2011 I will be a Medicare cardholder. It wasn't as difficult as it looked with all the paperwork I was receiving on a daily basis. Now I can scratch that off my list of things I had to do… on my own.

Showtime

On the night of what would be my last show with this studio, I had flashbacks of how it all began. Of how I saw the show for the first time back in 2005 and was mesmerized and just knew I had to join this dance studio. There were women my age dancing their hearts out and having the time of their lives up there on that stage. The people I met through dance will hold a special place in my heart. It was fun time; it was my time for me!

Before my last show I broke down and sent Dick an email letting him know I didn't have a problem if he wanted to come see me dance one last time. Of course I didn't let my gal pals know this; they would have slapped me silly. I had to listen to my heart on this one; he knew how important dancing was to me, so sending the email was justified in my mind. He always did take an interest in my love of dance. If he came I knew he would leave as soon as it was over, not wanting to face any of my family and friends that were there. How sad, he was always the perfect host to our group.

Friday night, June 24th, 2011. It's show time! As our group stood backstage my heart skipped a beat hoping he would be there watching. As we tapped out onto the stage, the second we turned to face the audience I immediately looked out over the top of everyone's head and caught a glimpse in the back of the packed auditorium of what I thought was his silhouette standing there. I somehow knew in my heart he would show. It didn't make me lose my focus; I wanted to dance my best since it was most likely going to be my last time on this stage. After the show two other people mentioned that he was there. I know when he left the auditorium there was a tug at his heart knowing it was my last show and he would never come to see me dance again; knowing that he would not be at the after party celebrating or giving me roses.

First Face-to-Face

I had to send him another text asking if he could meet me at a coffee house close by. I had mail for him and he had computer discs for me. I also wanted to discuss some kind of terms for living expenses for myself. We had never really discussed this when he moved out in April.

It was July 1st, I arrived first and I saw him pull in. I started to get butterflies in my stomach.

He took the sheet with my monetary requests written on it and shoved it in with his mail and never once looked at it or said anymore about it. I asked him what we needed to do with the house when I leave. He said to get tenants in there and rent it to collect money. He is always about the money, too bad he doesn't have any. Oh by the way, he is also a Certified Financial Planner. He sure didn't practice what he preaches when it came to us! It has been almost a year since we made a mortgage payment. He said I could probably live in it another year before the bank would kick me out. That's a comforting thought... not knowing from one day to the next if I would have a roof over my head.

I told him I was planning to be bi-coastal for a while. He didn't need to know my real plans; I don't know what he does or where he goes. I arranged for someone I trusted to come "house sit" for me while I'm back east. That's all he needs to know, for now. This way the house will be taken care of, the utilities will be paid and it won't get vandalized. It will keep him from taking it back and renting it to strangers and pocketing the money. I planned to be back in February and June of 2012. After that he can do what he wants with it.

The next day was his birthday; I did send him a text wishing him a happy birthday. I only cried once. Ever since the salt from my tears started to eat into the skin under my eyes, vanity took over and I didn't cry as much. This weekend was always special and filled with fun. It started with his birthday and went through to the Fourth of July parade we enjoyed every year and then it ended with a big barbeque at our home with family and friends.

The annual Fourth of July parade starts soon. This will be my last time to sit and watch the hometown parade that came to be something I looked so forward to every year. We would load the car with chairs, plenty of water, snacks, and a camera. And we would even bring the dogs too. I'm not bringing the dogs this year; it would be too much for me to handle them by myself.

I sat with Marlo and her family. The parade didn't have the excitement this year as in past years. It could have been my frame of mind I guess. Afterwards we had a cookout at Marlo and Dave's. It was quiet, nice and bittersweet. We are both saying good bye to events that were part of our lives living on the Bay. We now have to look forward to creating new memories in our new lives.

Arriving home after a nice long walk, I reflected on the day. It is sad knowing the fun times and holidays together are over. It's still difficult remembering all the good times we shared over the years.

Preparing for the Yard Sale

Who hasn't had a yard sale? This one has a lot of emotions attached to it. Preparing for a good yard sale is a lot of work. We all have junk to get rid of and I wanted the sale to have things other people could really use. I didn't realize how many glasses, dishes, knick knacks, pillows, small pieces of furniture, and candle holders I had accumulated over the years. Not to mention the clothes I had and didn't want or need anymore. Marlo and my two daughters-in-law will be helping me and also selling their own items. There is less than two weeks and I have to put ads in papers and on the internet, make signs, get stuff priced, and find tables to put my stuff on. When he walked out he left me with everything to do with as I pleased. After being together for sixteen years there was more than I realized I would be trying to sell.

I have my blue tape ready for pricing, now where to start. How did I acquire all this stuff? Was there not one souvenir store I passed on any of our vacations? I am having a difficult time parting with some of these things. I then tell myself, "You are starting a new chapter in your life and this is in the past". These things are part of the past and they need to go.

The first thing is to clean out the garage and make room for all the items; this is becoming a major event!

I'm already tired just thinking about it.

My Brother, my Rock

I don't know where to begin; not wanting to go beyond 1994 it is difficult without going back in time as a big sister. Tom was born just before my tenth birthday. I was in heaven. A baby, after being an only child, it would be fun to be a big sister. It was like a real live doll, feeding and dressing him and I loved pushing him in his carriage around Old Town Alexandria. There is NO WAY that could be done nowadays. We would be gone for hours stopping at the five and dime for a soda and grilled cheese sandwich. He was a dream come true for me, at first.

Like all babies and puppies, cute and cuddly when they are little, not so cute as they grow up. Once he got to the age where he was now my mother's pet, I didn't like him as much. To make things worse, as a teenager in junior high school, I had to walk home every day with my friends and take a detour to pick him up at the babysitter's. He was four, I was fourteen, and you can only imagine how humiliating that was for me. It wasn't bad enough I had to have him tag along everywhere we went, but he sucked his thumb and carried a dirty, smelly nasty pillow with him. It was then he earned the nickname "take your brother"! It was pretty much like that for a while, he told Mom everything my friends and I did or said. We were all on restriction most of the time thanks to his big mouth. One afternoon a bunch of us and "take your brother" were hanging out when we came upon the laundry room in our apartment complex. We took Tom and stuffed him in the dryer, we said if he tattled on us again we would bring him back and next time leave him there! Of course the second we walked in the door at home he couldn't wait to tell Mom what we did.

As an adult he traveled all over the world with his job. I didn't see much of him except off and on over the years when he would be back in the U.S. We became close again about ten years ago and have been there for each other ever since.

When he first met Dick they hit it off and became fast friends. I was glad there was a male influence in the mix. I had my girlfriends and daughters-in-law as my support system, Dick just had me. At the time there was a mutual respect between my brother and him and I felt good about the friendship they shared. Too bad it would soon end.

My brother is my rock star and my hero. If there was no

Tom I don't know where I would be right now. He stepped up to the plate and bought a home for us to share, including all three pets. Having limited income and nothing to fall back on it was just way too painful to stay in the bay area, even if I had a roommate. My roommate left me! There is only one other person in this world I could live with and that's my brother.

If ever there were two siblings alike it would be the two of us. If there is a pillow crooked on the couch, I have to fix it before I walk out the door; he is the exact same way. "Neat freaks" doesn't begin to explain it. I drive myself nuts sometimes. It beats the alternative. We also love our threads. We both have so many clothes I don't think in my lifetime I would wear them all and Tom is the same. I have always claimed to be a "clothes whore" and a "TV addict". I said it and I'm proud of it.

When I realized the marriage was over and we would be going our separate ways, my brother said it was time to look for a place we could share. It meant moving back to the east coast, I was coming home. I feel like I've come full circle moving back. It is a comforting feeling knowing the surroundings, having people there I've known a long time plus I have family there. My neighborhood in California always reminded me of where my grandparents lived in Virginia, the lovely older homes, it always made me feel warm and fuzzy. It's nice to have good memories.

Tom started looking at townhome rentals that would accommodate the two of us, my two dogs, and cat. That's a lot to ask anybody to take on. He found several places; some didn't like the idea of so many pets. My brother had also been going through a divorce. He and his ex-wife received a settlement from the house they owned and now instead of renting he decided to purchase a home for us.

He was searching for a townhome that would give us privacy and room for the dogs and all the furniture I would be brining from my house. Tom had a small furnished apartment and all of his furniture is at the cottage on the Chesapeake Bay, his weekend Shangri-La.

Weekly he would go out with his realtor then send me pictures and the specs on each place he thought we would both like. The day he walked into our home he knew immediately this was it. He sent me pictures right away and I also knew right away that this was the one.

It is in Virginia, not far from Washington, DC, and close to my brother's workplace. Our new home has miles of walking trails and is close to shopping, restaurants, movie theaters, beautiful lakes, and much more. The house is perfect, three stories, three bedrooms, two and a half baths, a deck off the kitchen, two patios and an open pit wood burning fireplace inside. This will be our new home; I know our mom is in heaven smiling at us taking care of one another.

Since Tom's furniture is at the cottage on Chesapeake Bay, the furniture I'm bringing with me will fill the new townhome. I know already that this home that we will share will be warm, inviting and filled with love, laughter and happy memories. Oh how proud Mom would be.

Divorce?

This is a word I never liked. Why does it have to exist? Why do so many of us get married so we can go through it? The dictionary describes it as "the legal dissolution of a marriage; a complete or radical severance of closely connected things". The divorce rate in America is higher than ever before. That is really sad. Tammy Wynette sang a song dedicated to it. So many other songs, books, movies, TV shows, theater, poems, all bring it to life. Not to mention how many people have experienced it not just once, but twice or more. It is an emotional roller coaster no matter what the reason or circumstances. It takes a toll on everyone involved.

Years ago when I would get an invitation to a wedding I would be so excited. The thought of a beautiful bride walking down the aisle to marry the man of her dreams. It was such a fairy tale comes true, most girls dream of the day it happens to them. The white dress and veil, flowers, bridesmaids, parties, showers, all the hoopla that goes into planning a wedding. The books on getting married are as plentiful as the ones on divorce. If the book stores put them side by side on the shelves I bet it would save couples a lot of money. Read the first one about getting married and all the costs. Then read the second one on divorce and where that leaves you. If you don't do the first then you don't have to go through the other. It seems like a no brainer to me!

We never argued until 2008. I used to tell him I would never give him a divorce because I didn't want him to marry someone else. I meant it, at the time. It has been the saddest time in my adult life since he left, it also has been the most relaxed I've felt in a long while. When you love the way we did it is heartbreaking when the arguing and name calling starts. Once he was gone the arguing, meanness and nastiness stopped. I didn't miss that part of us.

I have been to see my attorney twice since we decided to separate. She wants me to dissolve the marriage before I move back east. My heart isn't telling me that's what I need to do right now. I know we will never reconcile, that ship has sailed. I just hope we can come to an understanding of what we need to do right now. I have a huge hurdle ahead of me with my move and I don't feel like a divorce is something I want to deal with right now. They say the three most stressful things a person can do is… divorce, move, and change jobs. I will be doing all three all at once. God help me to be strong.

The Yard Sale

Saturday, yard sale time! "Oh my God is all I can say. People were everywhere. We opened the garage door at 7am. Two of us scurried up to the main corner to put out more signs. We advertised for a 9am - 4pm sale. I figured people would start showing up at 8am. But as soon as we opened the garage to place our items in the driveway people were already starting to arrive. People came in their pajamas! We sold most of the items in the early part of the day. There would be a lull from time to time then more people would arrive. My daughter-in-law and Marlo were as busy as I was. My two sons and my other daughter-in-law were there helping and keeping watch that no one got sticky fingers.

It was now lunch time and the boys went to pick up some Thai food for lunch. We drank four bottles of champagne while taking care of business. It turned out to be as much fun as it was exhausting. Making some extra cash was worth it. All the hard work paid off. However, I won't be doing another one any time soon! I do recommend having a sale in the spring and fall, it is a great time to purge! People buy anything and everything! What's the saying, "Someone's junk is another person's treasure". Well that is certainly true. Some things I would have easily thrown away were the things that people wanted most.

My goal was to clear a certain amount and I made my goal. It was a good day all around. All my proceeds are going towards my moving expenses. It is my plan to have movers take my belongings and car to the east coast while I rent a van and drive with my daughter-in-law and the pets across country. There is no way I could fly with three pets on my own and it would be much better to drive ourselves with the pets in tow and being able to stop each evening to relax at a hotel. I have a moving company stopping by on Friday to give me a quote for all the furniture and boxes that I need to have loaded onto a moving truck for the coast-to-coast move and they are also giving me a quote to move my car to the east coast. This will really help knowing how much I still need to save to cover my move.

After the sale was over, we then had to bring all the stuff that didn't sell back into the garage. I had some odds and ends, not much big stuff. We left items out on the curb and before we closed the garage we saw people rifling through it. Anything left will now go to Goodwill or homeless shelters.

We all went to our favorite Mexican restaurant in town for a margarita and a snack. Everyone was totally exhausted so we made it an early night. They dropped me off at the house around 6:30. I walked inside, went into the garage and started to cry uncontrollably, again. I had held it together all day, but fell to pieces when I got home by myself. It was very hard for me today to sell items that had such a special memory and meaning.

As I looked around at what was left from the yard sale it seemed so real that the walls of our beautiful home were truly crumbling. I came back into the house, played with the dogs and showered them with attention. Poor little things didn't know what was going on all day. We kept them secure out back with no access to the garage area. They could hear all the cars and strange people coming and going. It didn't take me long to go from a crying fool to an angry, hurt woman. When he moved out three months ago, he left with his clothes, a recliner, lamp and a bookcase. I told him to take anything he wanted… but he left it all with me to deal with. Sixteen years, now he decides it's over and he leaves me to deal with getting rid of his things! It is much healthier for me to be angry right now. He is a son-of-a-bitch in my mind today.

The end of a marriage is like the loss/death of a loved one. When the loved one has passed you know you will never see them again. Memories are what you have to remember. When they leave and there is a chance you will or can see them from time to time, all the feelings come to surface until that final stage of grief allows you to be free. You still go through the seven stages of grief: Shock/Disbelief, Denial, Anger, Bargaining, Guilt, Depression and Acceptance/Hope. So far I've experienced five; guilt hasn't been something I'm feeling, not yet. When I look back at our time together I feel as a wife, a friend, and a lover, I was always there for him; until he started working with her. Acceptance will be when I can close this chapter of my life; I am nowhere near that at the moment.

As I awoke the next morning I was in a real deep funk. This too shall pass. I just know the hardest part both mentally and physically is still ahead of me. My family and friends are there for me; they've got me this far. What would I do without them?

Health

I wasn't going to talk about this part of my life. However, it does have some insight to my story.

From the time I was seventeen, my senior year in high school, was the time when my health issues began to plague me for what would be the rest of my life.

It always seemed to be stomach related. I've had colon cancer and am fully recovered and thankful every day. There were other stomach related illnesses I also suffered from my entire adult life. Very, very painful issues. I have been through every test possible and I am checked on a regular basis every six months. Keeping healthy with exercise and understanding how important it is to watch the foods I eat has been key to my recovery from these stomach issues.

It was 1999 after undergoing some minor surgery and I just wasn't bouncing back the way the doctors were hoping I would. I was tired all the time, my energy level was nil and it was hard to get out of bed in the morning. My joints ached fiercely. I knew something wasn't right. My surgeon sent me to a specialist and after weeks of being poked and x-rayed they diagnosed me with Lupus. I knew little about it other than there was no cure.

Dick and I had been together four years by then and we were married at the time I was diagnosed. He didn't deal well with illness of any kind, but back then he showed concern as best he knew how. Diet, exercise, eating healthy and lots and lots of rest plus a medicine cabinet full of vitamins were the most important things for me to follow. One more thing, I have to limit my time in the sun. Having been a sun worshiper my entire life, this was going to be tough. It could have been worse, and again I was thankful.

May of 2005 I was retiring from my job in the city. It was bittersweet, however I knew it was time. My body needed a rest from the twelve hour days that began at 4am. I decided to get all my doctors' appointments taken care of before I went off the company's insurance program. First on my list was the dermatologist.

My doctor's appointment was routine; they took some skin scrapings, checked me over with the special light and gave me some "zaps" here and there and then sent me home. The next day I get a call and was told not to worry, but I needed to come back in ASAP and have a spot removed off my shoulder, it had come back as Melanoma.

My first response to the nurse on the other end of the phone was, "I am not going to miss my going away party at work, can we do this next week"? The answer I received was a polite yet forceful, "No". A couple days later I went to have this "spot" removed. The doctor's office was just a few blocks from where I worked. It was a nice walk and it gave me time to relax before my procedure. Dick and my friend Peg went with me for my appointment to offer their support. It was comforting for me knowing they were there in the lobby waiting for me. I was really scared; this form of cancer can be very deadly. All I could think about was the many hours I spent in the sun baking myself and years of going to the tanning salons, not to mention the terrible sunburns I had over the years.

The doctor had to literally dig into my shoulder to retrieve the entire tumor that was growing. He asked if I wanted to see what he found. I did look and it was at that moment I knew my sun worshiping days were over forever.

November 2010. One of my yearly tests showed I had some "pre-cancer" cells. They were showing up around my breast area. This could have been residual from the Melanoma spot I had removed five years earlier. After an MRI the doctor wanted to do a few radiation treatments on me just to be on the safe side.

This was during the time Dick decided to move out of our bedroom and told me he didn't want to be married anymore. Feeling more alone than ever, If I ever needed his support it was right now. I told him what the doctor had found and what they were planning to do. He didn't say much and he didn't ask any questions. It was like I had given him some information about a complete stranger. He showed no concern or compassion whatsoever. I could literally feel the knife being twisted into my heart.

During the treatments my friends and family were there for me as always. Radiation treatment is hard on a body and it weakened me also. There were times that all I could do was lie on the couch cuddled with the dogs and sleep. Dick was still in the house and saw what I was going through. But did he ever once offer to get me a glass of water or ask how I was doing? No! Not once! I was getting the final test results back from the doctor the day after Dick moved his things from the house. Everything is okay and all my tests came back clean. He knew when I was getting my test results back, however to this day he has NEVER asked me what those results were. This just goes to show how empty and heartless he became. Not once did he ask how I was doing, if I needed anything, NOTHING. I sometimes wonder how I loved this man, who has become a complete stranger to me, for so many years.

I can honestly say since we are no longer together I feel better than I have in years. I used to tell him, especially towards the end of our marriage, that he was the reason I was sick all the time. I truly believe that. The mental stress and torture were having a direct effect on my physical health. He was literally sucking the life out of me.

Where Will the Money Come From?

The medical bills keep piling up, the bill collectors keep calling, and I'm late on my utilities. Why can't he help me just a little? I sent him copies of all the extras that I had to pay in June, and not one response at all from him. His way has always been to put things on a back burner and it will just go away. My ex-boss always said, "It's cheaper to keep her". How right he was. Dick knows he will have to pay me spousal support for some time or until I re-marry. And trust me, that isn't going to happen at my age.

My cousin was visiting from the east coast. What an inspiration she has been, it was like the lights finally went on. She and I talked and talked about my situation, one that she knew all too well as she went through her separation and divorce years ago. I listened to her words of wisdom and started to follow through with her advice. When I finally stopped crying it started to make sense what she was saying. There were steps I had to take before I left

California and time was getting short. She made me see that I didn't need him anymore and that I could only rely on myself, friends, and family. The only things I want from him are what I am entitled to. All he is to me now is a check I receive two times a month.

I received my quote from the movers and I almost had a heart attack right there on the kitchen floor! The quote was $10,400 with a full pack; $8,700 just to move the furniture and boxes and $1,700 to move my car. That didn't include me renting a minivan to drive with the pets and my daughter-in-law. Plus food, gas, and lodging; there was no way I could or would be able to have this be my way of transportation back to the east coast. I had another long distance mover give me a quote and it was even higher. It was time for Plan B.

As soon as I could a call was made to rental truck companies to get quotes for the truck, car carrier and a gas estimate. With what I was planning to move with me they said it would take 26-foot diesel truck to load it all. I reserved the truck and decided to have a family-owned car carrier take the car out east for me instead of pulling it behind the big moving truck. Now I have found someone I can trust to drive this behemoth truck across country with me and my three pets in the front cab.

This week was a step towards what will happen next, cutting my costs. I feel like now that the transportation across country has been taken care of, there are other pieces of my life I have to look after. I now have my own car insurance policy, dropping my monthly premium by a significant amount. One of my larger hospital bills sent me a letter stating they had adjusted my invoice to "hardship full write off". What a blessing! As of August 1ˢᵗ I will no longer have my land phone line. This is the first time in my entire life I have not had a land line phone. I couldn't take another call from creditors; I gave them all Dick's office and cell number. Call him, not me; he can deal with it since it is his mess. Last thing I did was make the appointment with my attorney to finally dissolve the marriage before I leave. That was the hardest thing I did this week. It is one step and one day at a time.

Having family and friends this week helped me move to the next steps I need to take to end my life as it is now and move forward with my new life back east.

Dissolution of the Marriage

It was like any other day. I didn't feel sad and I wasn't doubting my decision to do what needed to be done. I never wanted a divorce; it's just the way it is. I sat down and made my list of items I wanted to address with my attorney. I still can't believe it has come to this. I didn't ask for much and was more than fair with my terms. My attorney advised me to ask for Dick to pay for my moving costs since it was his fault I had to move in the first place. There was no way I could afford to stay in California on my minimal income. She was right and it only seemed fair. Besides, I would have moved anyway even if it weren't a financial issue. It is just way too painful to be anywhere that we were together and everywhere I went were ghosts and too many memories.

We filled out the paperwork to be filed with the court. For some strange reason I was without any emotion as we completed the details. Maybe I was just too numb to realize that almost sixteen years together were truly over. I guess the reality still hadn't sunk in.

Driving back to work after visiting with my attorney, I walked into the office and suddenly it felt like a ton of bricks had been lifted off my shoulders. I didn't feel sad, I didn't feel happy; I felt lighter.

The man I fell in love with was gone, I just haven't fallen out of love with him yet. "Bittersweet" is used a lot in my vocabulary, along with "one day at a time". I am finally starting to look forward to beginning my new life. It's hard to let go of the past though. When you get to be my age you want to look forward and not back. Things are finally starting to come together.

I kept wondering when the tears would start again after deciding to dissolve our marriage. It didn't hit me until I received my paperwork in the mail from my attorney. Reading the words in black and white made it all seem so real. I don't have to say what came next, lots and lots of tears. I was hoping I had finished crying over this man. Every time I cry he wins, so I have to stop. It isn't good for me or any of the people around me that are trying to help me get through this difficult time in my life.

As I stated before, I didn't ask for much; he doesn't have anything left to give. I sure as hell didn't want any part of his company as long as she was attached to it. I would rather stick a pin in my eye than have her be associated to anything with my name on it. He has until the fifteenth of August to reply to my requests. If not we go to court and I really don't think he wants to do that.

It was a week ago today I filed the final papers; haven't heard one word from him. For some reason I thought he might call. I'm sure he was waiting for me to do this so he didn't have to. Sixteen years and this is what it comes to. So many of us know the empty, sick, sad, lonely, and broken feeling I'm going through. And it sucks!

I went to a seminar with my friend Marlo last night. It was very eye-opening. I understand why she has been part of this organization for so long. Each person attending last night had something to walk away with. Mine was, "I will have a magnificent life". I have to believe this. No one needs a man or woman to make them a better person; we do that on our own.

August 15th, the best part of today was that my son was born thirty six years ago. I can remember the day like it was yesterday. It was one of the happiest moments of my life. Today is also the deadline for Dick to respond to my requests filed in the divorce papers.

It finally came... the email from my attorney with Dick's response. He did agree to what I asked, however, he wanted me to quit claim the house to him and he only wanted to pay my spousal support for five years. Now you know that wasn't going to happen!

Do you Believe in Guardian Angels?

I usually don't work on Fridays. There was a reason I was at my desk the day a gentle man with a kind face and lovely smile walked in the door. He said he was new to the area and was looking for information on where to go and what to see. My place of business had that information at his fingertips.

We started talking and I felt like I had known him my entire life. I found myself sharing my pain of the past four years with him. We talked about my move and my book; he talked to me in a way that made sense. He said I was a brave, strong woman starting out on a brand new journey like I was. He said my story would reach out and help many others going through a similar situation. It was not how he expressed his beliefs, it was the way he expressed himself. I found myself hanging on his every word. As he spoke I could hear nothing but positive energy coming from his soul. I asked was he a minister or an inspirational speaker.

He said he likes to inspire people because it makes him a better person. I found myself believing everything he offered through our conversation.

Ever since my brief encounter with this man my frame of mind has been so much more positive. I'm not afraid to make this long trip across country. I'm not scared to start a new life at my age. I will be fine, better than fine. He said while on my journey don't stop and look back, it will only slow me down. Our conversation had left me at peace for the first time in a long time. It is a nice feeling.

I can honestly say I was a little sad that Dick didn't even call to ask if a divorce is what I really wanted. Part of me hopes his heart is also broken when he thinks about what we had and are now losing. There were some pretty special times. I'll be able to smile one day when I think back on the good years we had together. There were more good years than years of falling apart.

I am stronger and able to stand on my feet again. I always could, although it was nice to have someone to lean on so the weight was only on one foot. I didn't do any of this alone; my family and friends were there to help keep me strong.

Trip Planning in the Works

There is nothing easy about a move. My move is taking me from the San Francisco Bay area to the east coast just outside Washington, DC. I had reserved a 26-foot diesel truck and made arrangements for my car to be transported separately. All I need now is to find someone that can drive the truck for me; it definitely wasn't going to be me! I knew I couldn't handle that monster.

So far, the couple of people I have asked either had a schedule conflict with the move dates or were too afraid to drive such a huge truck across country. The second I mentioned my driver dilemma to Rachel she didn't hesitate to volunteer. So I am flying my best friend from Florida to drive us cross country. We will make it an adventure for sure and hope for the best. Thelma and Louise ride again!! I have an agency mapping our route out for us and reserving nightly hotel rooms that accommodates pets. Hopefully it won't be too hard on the pets. Before we leave I will get tranquilizers for the dogs just in case. I might get them for me also!

Rachel assures me she can do this. Having driven her SUV with a thirty-foot camper on the back, I am taking her at her word. I pray every day for us and the long 3,000 miles across country with all my possessions. We are going to document the trip and I will put the journey in my book as we start our drive across the United States.

This will be my third cross country trip, having driven it twice before it doesn't seem so scary. The map and route I received is extremely detailed and I think we will be fine. We can do it! Like I said in the beginning of the book, you can do whatever you want once you set your mind to it.

Packing is not my favorite part of the move, unpacking is. I walk from room to room every day and just take in every last minute of the way it was. I look forward to making it the way it will be. I'm leaving all the pictures of the two of us behind. No reason to bring them, it's not like I'm going to sit and go down memory lane looking at them any time soon.

Got up this morning and packed six boxes and already I am exhausted. I only have a hundred more to go! Not really, but it seems like it will take a hundred boxes for all my stuff. Where did it all come from? Five weeks until I start my trip across this beautiful country we live in. I am going to take advantage of every single minute of it. Some people never leave the town they were born in. I feel fortunate this is my fourth trip driving from coast to coast. This time will hopefully be my last time moving furniture!

Today was difficult. Seeing the house filling up with boxes, the walls are bare, and different items stacked up against the walls. I always thought leaving this house we would do together. Most of my top floor is now packed. I'm trying to keep the boxes out of the way so there is some kind of organization, if that is even possible, while the house is being turned upside down.

I had to stop packing and running up and down the steps, my chest started feeling tight so it was time for a break. I called to confirm the reservations for the truck and the auto carrier and bought Rachel's airline tickets from Tampa to San Francisco then from Virginia back to Tampa. Things are starting to come together. As painful as everything has been I feel so much stronger and feel like I have accomplished something big on my own. We can do whatever we set our minds to, I truly believe this.

I did not think I would be doing this again, however I still have things I need to try and sell and a yard sale seemed to work. So this Saturday I will try one more time to sell some more items and make some more cash to put towards the move. Things that are left to sell I have no emotional ties to; hopefully someone else will want them.

Well, I didn't do as well as last time but I still did fair. I packed up the leftovers and took a box of nicer clothes to a consignment store and another box went to charity. Each day is getting a little less heartbreaking for me. I knew this when I woke up one morning knowing I didn't want to be here anymore. It is just way too painful for me.

My brother has already moved into the beautiful townhome and is making a few minor repairs. He always did like doing things around the house; all his homes were picture perfect.

Starting to Forget

Every time I pack a box it makes it easier for me to get over him. Since he left the house with only a few items, it is up to me to sort through all of it and pack the boxes. First I had to get the boxes, and they don't come cheap. So one afternoon after work and while still in my dressy work clothes, I saw a pile of really nice boxes stacked neatly by a dumpster. I pulled my car over, got out, and started piling the boxes in the trunk. You could tell they had just been set out as they were dry and clean. Well, except for a little dust and getting a little sand in my shoes. It was the last box that threw me over the edge. I picked it up and a rat ran across my foot. That was it! I drove home as fast as I could, my shoes went in the trash right away and I took a hot shower, all the while cursing the day I met him after that. He has no idea what he has put me through, nor does he care.

Dealing with all the aftermath of him, each day gets easier for me to forget him. Dick has been gone almost five months now. The last time we saw each other was July 1st, it is now September.

I went to my attorney the other day to finalize what I was asking for. He wanted to only pay my spousal support for five years! That wasn't going to happen, so we changed that part. He also wanted me to quit claim the house to him, which I agreed to, but only after the divorce is final in February. My moving expenses have now increased by two thousand dollars. My attorney is asking him to pay all moving costs. Now is the waiting game for his response. It is Labor Day weekend so we might not hear from him until Tuesday. I know he does not want to go in front of a judge to be told what he should or should not be responsible for. He hates being told what to do and he knows my case is strong because my attorney will justify the "abandonment card" and the judge will shame him into everything I am asking and then some if he tries to fight me. California is a 50/50 state and by law I could get half of his business and everything else. Why would I want any part of what has caused me so much heartache, he can keep his damn business.

I'm starting to forget the sound of his voice. He has a gentle tone, very soothing. I remember when he used to read his huge law books to me when I couldn't fall asleep. He would spoon with me until I fell asleep while reading pages of boring legal mumble jumble; it always worked.

Going through the desks and drawers of the furniture I am finding so many more memories. Our marriage license, the silk flowers from our wedding, pictures from Puerto Rico, Hawaii, Las Vegas, New York, New Orleans, and so many other wonderful trips we shared together. What am I supposed to do with the pictures and trip memorabilia now? Keep it? Throw it away? Pack it all in the bottom of a box? What do I do with all the things that were us for sixteen years? Will there be a day when I can look at the pictures and have fond memories? Well definitely not right now. So I set aside a box of all the pictures of us together to deal with at another time.

Three weeks until my big move. There is so much to still take care. My house is in shambles, but I just have to get over it and deal somehow. It is temporary and will soon be unpacked and put away in our new place.

Daily paperwork about an auction or foreclosure on the house arrives in the mail. How sad. In my heart I know he wanted this all along. When he decided the house was upside down I know she talked him into letting it go. There was never going to be a loan modification like we discussed and began paperwork on. Their intention was for me to leave so he could move back in. There was no way I was going to let that happen, or so I thought. Screwed again by him with no satisfaction.

It is Sunday and I'm going to church. It will be good to reflect and be thankful for all I have and what is yet to come. Being raised a Catholic in the 60's it was a sin to do almost anything. I remember going to confession and spending another half hour saying penance for all my sins. You would always see your Catholic friends from school doing the same. The longer they sat the more sins they committed! Not that I didn't like being brought up in the Catholic religion; I attended St. Mary's Academy in Alexandria, VA. It was a beautiful school and we were taught by The Sisters of the Holy Cross. My first grade Nun passed away half-way through the year and we were all made to attend Mass with her lying there in her habit in an open casket at the altar. That was the first time I had ever seen a dead person. It was disturbing, to say the least.

Not to get off the subject, but the church I am attending now is a non-denominational church. I wish I had that option long ago. If I had, religion would have been a more important part of my life. Leaving church now I feel a sense of peace. I don't go every Sunday, but when I do go it gives me a good feeling.

Each day I miss him less and worry about him more. He had the potential to successfully do and go wherever he wanted and he blew it. With having literally no contact with Dick in such a long time, I don't know where his mind set is now. We used to be able to finish each other's sentences; she now seems to be doing that for him.

Three Weeks Until the Move

So many things still left to do. The house is a mess; something I just have to overlook for the time being. Boxes and stuff are stacked everywhere. I keep walking by one box and can hear the clock inside ticking… that's a little scary. I am trying my best to keep the pets comfortable, especially my kitty. Cats are very in tune with anything out of the ordinary and I can tell the poor little guy is stressed, scared, and confused with all the changes going on in the house. My part time job was over and I now had a couple of weeks to totally concentrate on the move and saying my good-byes.

Friday September 9th he calls me back from a message I had left the day before regarding some mail he had received at he house. It was the first time we spoke on the phone in almost two months. He wanted me to "quit claim" the house over to him. I had been receiving so much advise as to what to do that my head was spinning. I know it will short-sale, it is supposed to go up for auction December 7th, our wedding anniversary. The only thing I didn't want was for him to move back and bring his "people" with him into what was once our home. Hasn't he slapped me in the face enough? I would hope he would have enough feeling left not to screw me over again. We have decided to meet Sunday to discuss some things before I leave. I didn't think I would see him again; maybe this will give me some closure.

It is now Sunday September 11th, our first time seeing each other in months. He was sitting in his car when I arrived. As soon as I saw him my heart started to beat faster. He asked me to sit in the car so we could talk. I had paperwork he needed to see and some personal items I needed to give him. He didn't look good to me. His color was ashen, he needed a haircut and I could tell from the way the buttons on his shirt were pulling that he was heavier in the tummy. It was the first time since he left five months ago that we had a civil conversation with each other.

I always loved his hands. They were soft, yet strong, and made me feel safe and secure when he touched me. I asked if I could hold his hand and he put it there for me. We just sat and held hands and I stroked his arm as we both cried. I wanted to scoop him up and tell him everything would be okay and that I would take care of him and make everything alright. I had to be strong and keep remembering what he has put me through the past couple of years. My heart was breaking all over again.

He did offer me good advice on several things in question. He gave me the paperwork to quit claim the house. I am so over the letters from the bank and since it is going up for public auction in December, I decided I don't want any part of it. So I told him I would sign the quit claim papers. He will never make any money on the house so I was fine with letting it go. It doesn't mean anything to me anymore. He is trying to keep it from going into foreclosure to avoid the taxes that will eat him alive. He said the best thing he could try and do is work with the bank and do a loan modification and rent it out to make the house payment. I have a lady living in the house with me now. His plan all along was to have me leave so he could move back into the house so he didn't have to pay rent.

I did ask him to keep his business partner out of the house even though it won't be mine anymore. Out of respect for me I would hope he would keep his word. He always did in the past. I found out later that only lasted two days from the time I left. He had her at the house two days later. Bastard! He is a snake in the grass; I am seeing his true colors more and more every day.

September 24th

Oops he did it again! Yes, it is my birthday. He completely forgot my birthday last year and we had the biggest fight of our lives that evening. Well, this year was better without him there. However, he was supposed to give me my money by now for the move and also pay my attorney's fees. I am leaving in four days and now out of nowhere he wants to go to court because I want to revisit my spousal support terms after six years. He said he doesn't want to pay me for the rest of his life so we will now let a judge make that decision. I am not asking to be paid for the rest of my life. I think he owes it to me to pay me for more than the five years he has decided on. He knows the California laws; how stupid does he think I am?

I am so ready to go in front of a judge with my story and bring my witnesses that will testify on my behalf. I told him to bring it on! I had so much to say and "my" people would be behind me 100%. The advice he has given friends and clients would make your head spin. This is where her nasty, manipulative self comes into play. He was never like this before. He was always moral and fair and possessed high standards. Not anymore! I am leaving with everything I own in four days and he now pulls this out of his bag of tricks.

I called him today to ask why he was doing this to me at the eleventh hour. He said, "Ask your former ex-husband for spousal support since he too promised to take care of you for the rest of your life". It was like talking to a complete stranger. Two weeks ago after our first conversation in five months, he was giving me good advice that made sense, holding my hand and crying. And now this?! I don't think he has the money to pay me for my moving expenses, spousal support or my attorney's fees, so this is a delay tactic on his part. This is the way he is now, not the way he was when we married almost fifteen years ago. Every word that comes out of his mouth has her verbiage on it. I never wanted any of this. After driving five days in a truck with three animals and then unpacking, the last thing I want to do is get on a plane and fly back to appear in court with his sorry ass. He makes me sick every time I have to deal with him now. I know she is behind every move he makes.

My birthday turned out to be a great day. There was a big party for me at my favorite restaurant with my friends, family and the people I have become acquainted with over the past nine years were there to wish me well. It was good to see everyone laughing and having a good time. He wasn't mentioned or missed at all. Earlier in the day he tried to ruin it with a phone call and I would have none of it.

I am all packed and ready to go. I can't get on the road soon enough. My time here has come to an end. When I walk out the door on Thursday I will never look back, only forward.

It's Time – the Move

Wednesday, September 28th. Well, the time has finally arrived. Garage sales are over. Everything I own has been packed and loaded onto the 26-foot moving truck, now nicknamed, "The Beast". Well, almost everything I own. Some items were given away at the last minute when I realized they would not fit onto the truck after all. Damn him to hell! It is starting to sting in bits and pieces all over again during these last 24 hours before my departure from the place I love the most in this world. Having to give away or sell items I have treasured and loved for so long, all because it won't fit into the moving truck. When I first saw The Beast I thought for sure it would hold all my precious belongings and treasures – my life. Professional packers came to pack it all up and I was shocked when it would not all fit. Now I must decide on what pieces of furniture or other items I must now leave behind. This is his entire fault! Lord help me to get through this. This is hands down the hardest thing I have experienced in my life so far. The house, our beautiful love-filled home, is completely bare. Nothing but a couple of small air mattresses in the master bedroom for Rachel and me to sleep on the last night in my home. My overnight bag, a couple small boxes, and a small cooler are all that's left to go on the truck.

I am beginning to literally feel such a pain in my chest. Pure heartache! That's what this pain is. Complete loss and fear all rolled up into one huge knot that has punched a hole in my heart the size of Texas! The memories, both good and bad, are all of a sudden overwhelming me in flashes as I walk from room to room mentally saying goodbye. One moment standing quietly with tears streaming down my face, the next moment crying in a ball on the floor. Then there were the moments of reality and anger setting in. I cursed him occasionally under my breath and in the very next moment whispered how much I had loved him, and still do. I have had my heart broken before, but it never felt as truly devastating as this. The dogs and cat are feeling the loss too. They are shadowing my every move, following me everywhere and acting very anxious. You can tell how confused and lost they are with all their furniture and beds and toys gone. Once again I curse him under my breath not only for my suffering, but for the pets and others his actions have affected. Does he have any idea the devastation he has caused? The devastation SHE has caused? Not just to me, but to all those who cared about him. My friends became his friends and now they were just as hurt by his actions as I was. I wonder to myself if they can sleep well at night. Of course they can. I know neither of them has a conscience. She is a driven, selfish, cold-hearted bitch and he is her puppet. His heart has turned to stone. Marlo once said to me, "He has no heart, he always used yours".

Well, it's time now to go pick up Rachel from the airport. I can't wait to see her and hold her tightly to me. Talking to her almost daily and then some throughout this whole ordeal has been a lifeline to me. She too has been on this emotional roller coaster with me all the while being on her own roller coaster ride dealing with her ex and custody issues for the last three years. We have been more than rocks of strength to one another; boulder might be a better description. Maybe mountains of strength is an even better description. But actually having her here next to me while I am about to leave my dream life, well, words escape me of the depth of our friendship and what it means to me.

I am waiting just inside the entrance doors at the airport when I see my girl coming down the ramp. She hasn't spotted me yet but her long blonde hair stands tall above all others. I immediately have a flashback to the first time I saw her nearly 22 years ago. Tall, blonde and pretty and with that certain aura about her that when people saw her from across the room they just knew that she was sweet, kind, and loving. She is that and so much more. From several yards away Rachel has finally seen me. She picks up her pace now and heads straight for me. The look on her face is of mixed emotions, I can tell. We both are thinking the same thoughts at this very moment. In the past fifteen years every time Rachel came to visit me it was for pure pleasure and joy. Now, we both knew this time was not an arrival to celebrate a holiday or special event, but one of sadness and heartache. We would not be taking long walks with the dogs down by the marina. We would not be going to my favorite Mexican restaurant to hang with the gang. We would not be going into the city to walk the Golden Gate Bridge or down to the Haight where Rachel loved to shop among the hippies. We were not going to a Twilight movie opening or a Twilight convention. No, this was a sad visit indeed.

I was frozen still right where I stood and could not move my legs to approach her. I was overcome with emotion and we both saw the tears streaming down each other's faces from several feet away. We did not speak. We did not have to. Rachel is several inches taller than me and her long arms had now engulfed me in an embrace that lasted for what seemed like several minutes. I could feel myself just letting go and falling into her embrace with emotion and relief. Neither of us could let go of one another and when we did it was then that Rachel cupped my face in her hands, looked me straight in the eye and whispered to me, "everything is going to be just fine, Hon". That's what we call each other, "Hon". We embraced once again and then left the airport.

It only took a few minutes to get to the house. From the outside nothing looked changed. But once you walked inside the front door, it was all changed. The hollow emptiness now caused an echo in every room. The wheels of Rachel's suitcase ticked across the tile floor of the now empty living room and it sounded so loud to me. The sound stopped and I turned around to see Rachel frozen in the middle of the room with shock and emotion on her face and slowly shaking her head while her eyes took in the emptiness. All my beautiful furniture and décor were gone. Sold, given away, or loaded on the Beast now. She looked at me and all I could say was, "I know, I know". We walked upstairs to the master bedroom with the air mattresses on the floor with sheets and blankets and pillows. "That is just like you", Rachel said. "Even with air mattresses you have made them up to look so nice and welcoming like a damn five star hotel". "Is that a mint I see on the pillow"? We both burst into laughter and went back downstairs.

We went to the back patio area where Rachel played with the dogs in the beautiful dusk setting. Again, I could tell that she too was running through bittersweet and fun memories of the many cookouts and parties we had in the backyard. The hammock, chairs, tables, benches, grill and fountain were all gone now. It too was as bare as the inside of the house. We didn't stay out there very long. We went into the kitchen where Rachel made her famous chicken salad for our road trip. We sipped on ice cold sweet tea and were pretty quiet for awhile. We took the dogs for a quick walk up and down the main street and came back in to settle for the night. We headed upstairs with the dogs and cat in tow and lay down on the air mattresses. I had left a dresser with a TV on it and we watched a few of our favorite shows. I don't know when we fell asleep. I just remember waking up before sunrise.

Thursday, September 29th. The big day. I headed downstairs and let the dogs out. Rachel soon followed. A couple of the neighbors had come over to help with the last few items to be loaded onto the truck and to say goodbye. We were all putting on brave faces but we all knew the enormous sadness that was surrounding us that morning. Rachel was outside checking out the truck and getting herself familiar with its size and functions and arranging the mirrors. We had taken our suitcases out as the last items to put on the back of the truck. The cab had a bench seat but very little storage space. We limited ourselves to our purses, the cooler and a small bag with crackers and snacks. And of course we had the pet items and beds arranged. A bed under the seat for the cat and a bed setup between Rachel and me for the dogs. Of course, I knew that at any given time all three of the animals would be in either one of our laps during the trip.

The previous year I had collected two six-foot cardboard cutouts of our favorite Twilight characters. Edward for Rachel and Carlisle for me. I had folded them in half and stood them up behind the bench seat of the cab to look like they were riding with us. I mean, here we are, two women, brave yet all alone, making a cross country trip. We figured if people didn't think we were alone then they wouldn't mess with us. Of course, Rachel entertained the idea of bringing a gun. She jokingly said she was afraid she might use it on Dick and Puki before we left and then where would we be?

We both went back into the house for a quick bathroom run before heading out. Rachel went upstairs to the master bath, but I just stayed downstairs and used the guest bath. It was time. I gathered up the pets and headed out to the truck. I didn't prolong it at all. With the house being empty the last couple of days I had realized that what made it a home was the loving couple and their belongings that lived in it. All of that was gone and it was just an empty structure to me now. The emotional attachment was suddenly gone. I had accepted it and was ready to go. My neighbor helped me into the truck and handed the dogs and cat to me one by one. I had fleeting visions of Noah's Ark. I closed the door and rolled down the window to speak to my neighbors one last time. We said our goodbyes and then I look up to see Rachel heading towards the truck with the biggest shit-eatin' grin on her face. I wasn't quite sure why she was grinning so big, but she seemed excited and ready to go. She climbed into The Beast and asked my neighbor to take a picture of us. He took her camera and went to the front of the truck and snapped a couple of pictures. There we were, Rachel, me the pets, Edward and Carlisle.

I looked at Rachel and asked her how she was feeling and if she was comfortable with the truck. She assured me she was and looked at me and paused. "I think it would be a good idea if we said a little prayer every morning before we start driving". So we did. Rachel led the prayer each time and it was short and sweet. "Dear Lord, please protect us during this journey and help us to arrive safely to our destination each night". She put the truck in gear and we were off!

Now, Rachel and I have been on too many road trips to count. Needless to say, our nicknames are appropriately, "Thelma and Louise". We love our road trips and always have fun and laugh until we almost pee our pants. And this trip, although not such a happy one, I knew would be fun anyway. I was amazed at Rachel's calm and relaxed demeanor as we drove through the narrow streets of town heading to the interstate. Seriously, this beast of a truck was scary. Rachel had experience towing a 30-foot pop-up camper with her SUV, but this sucker was tall, long and packed to the hilt. There was no rearview mirror as the truck was taller than the cab and so we could only see via the side mirrors. Rachel had prepared me for the kind of co-pilot she would need on this trip. There would actually be times that I might have to stick my head and then some outside my door window just to make sure everything was clear for us to move. She had asked me before the trip to make sure that I found hotels that she could just park and easily drive through or circle the parking lots, as she was not comfortable with backing up in reverse with The Beast.

As we entered onto the interstate I realized that although I was a bit teary-eyed pulling away from the house, I did not look back once and had not burst into an emotional breakdown. I stayed stronger than ever. At this point I was literally cried out and was distracted being a co-pilot and tending to the pets. I had obtained tranquilizers from the vet for each of them. They had never been on such a long ride and I wasn't sure how this trip was going to affect them. Especially being in a different hotel room for the next few nights. I didn't let Rachel know, but even though I trusted her completely with driving The Beast, I was scared to death anyway! It didn't take me long to relax as Rachel proved herself to be a great driver of this monstrosity. She handled the truck with ease and had coached me well on the importance of communication between pilot and co-pilot. Most importantly, that I would need to be her extra set of eyes for reading road signs and being alert to all the other traffic and vehicles around us.

This was not a sight-seeing trip either. Although we knew that we would be driving through some beautiful areas of the country that I had seen before but she had not, Rachel knew we were on a tight schedule for the next five days and we could not stop to take pictures, sight see or bask in the beauty of our beautiful country. Therefore, all pictures taken would be from the windows as we passed by. We were on a mission! Rachel had to be on a flight back home on the night of the fifth day of travel. This meant we had to travel a minimum of 12-14 or more hours each day. I could not drive the truck at all and Rachel would be doing all the driving. We had to limit ourselves to how much we drank and ate each day so we would not have to stop too often. We would only stop to gas up the truck, walk the dogs and bathroom breaks. Rachel pumped gas while I walked the dogs and then we took turns watching the pets while we each took a bathroom break and then we'd hit the road again. It was teamwork at its best. The dogs took turns snuggling up to each of us and laying in our laps. The cat pretty much stayed in his little nest beneath the seat and only came out occasionally to check things out. Every few hours I would fill up their water bowl as we were driving to refresh them. I limited their food and water intake as well as we did not have the time to spare on extra potty breaks for them. Rachel and I survived on water and snacks of crackers and chicken salad. Only eating small amounts and drinking very little. At our age, we too could not afford the extra amounts of water we were used to drinking or we would have been stopping every two hours. Rachel had only one request for a beverage other than water for this trip and that was Red Bull. She wanted to stay alert and knew that would do the trick. I had bought an entire case of it! The large size ones! I too wanted to make sure she stayed awake and alert.

At the first stop for gas as I was climbing into The Beast, I saw that Rachel had begun to wallpaper the entire cab with beautiful color pictures of all our favorite Twilight characters and images from our favorite scenes in the movies. It was her goal to create a mural from top to bottom inside the cab to keep our minds from wandering off into dark places. She had brought the last book of the series on CD for us to listen to during the trip. It was amazing and it worked. It was so nice to listen to the CD's and look around to have a visual of the characters. There were pictures taped on the ceiling, the doors and the dash. She continued this at every stop until the entire cab was wallpapered. We were in our own little Twilight paradise.

I giggled and told her I loved it. We felt like silly teenagers again. As we were pulling out of the station I suddenly remembered about her big grin when she had exited the house earlier that morning. I asked her what it was all about. She suddenly had the grin on her face again and proceeded to tell me why. She said she had purposely gone to the master bedroom before we left because she wanted to leave Dick a little treat. She knew he had been ever so anxious for me to move so he could get back into the house for himself. She despised him for all the heartache and pain he had caused me. At first she said she had thought about writing something on the bathroom mirror with her lipstick but had not brought it upstairs with her. She proceeded to tell me that after she used the bathroom and was walking out the doors, it struck her to go into the walk-in closet and pee on the carpet just below where Dick's clothes would hang once he moved back in. She was hoping it would leave an odor for weeks to come and he would not be able to figure out where it was coming from. She said she knew it was totally ridiculous and that because she had already gone to the bathroom it was too late to do it. But for a brief moment it gave her satisfaction just the thought of it. For just a split second I was surprised and she immediately apologized. I then burst into laughter as I told her it was perfectly ok, as I had taken some of the dogs' poop from that morning and had tossed it into the storage area under the stairwell hoping for the same outcome. She laughed even harder and told me on the way out she just looked at how sad and empty my beautiful dream home was now and she just wanted to do something to annoy the hell out of Dick just a little. So she proceeded to tell me that she had taken all the expensive light bulbs out of the dining room chandelier and had thrown them in the trash. He's so lucky she didn't bring a gun! I laughed even more as I told her how I used a black permanent marker to write a little personal message of my own on the white walls of the garage that would now have to be painted over with several coats of paint as it was quite large. A small inconvenience for him to repair, compared to the enormous inconveniences he had caused me. We had tears rolling down our faces we were laughing so hard. Rachel asked me to hand her a Red Bull and we were off!

We were able to stay at really nice, pet-friendly hotels each night. They offered continental breakfasts every morning that were perfect and fit into our diet and schedule. Of course, each night we looked like the Beverly Hillbillies as we made numerous trips out to The Beast to unload our suitcases, the cooler, the pets and their supplies, which included bags of cat and dog food, their bowls, a litter box and a bag of litter. Plus other items like my tablet, cell phones, chargers, etc. The truck was always parked far away from our actual room as it was so big and had to be parked where it fit best and where Rachel could easily drive out the next morning. And as is our luck, there were a few catastrophes along the way. Like on the third night when the huge, three foot glass container filled to the top with my matchbook collection had somehow broken, or shattered I should say, into smithereens. It was sitting at the very back next to the door of the truck and somehow got crushed. I had it loaded last and thought it was secure and padded enough. But I guess with the few bumps in the road we hit things somehow had shifted. Rachel and I both cut our fingers trying to clean up the mess. I was becoming increasingly agitated and pissed and Rachel was trying her best to salvage the matchbooks. We were both so exhausted and hungry and I told her to just forget it and we would throw it all away the next morning. The glass shards were all imbedded and mixed in with the matchbooks and I just didn't care anymore. But Rachel knew me better. She knew I had spent many, many years collecting those matchbooks from every place and restaurant I ever went to. She told me to let her handle it and to just go into the room and relax. I didn't even have the energy to argue with her. She is a Taurus and stubborn as hell sometimes and when she wants to take care of something like this, she will not give up.

Several minutes later she walked into the room. She was obviously having a hot flash as her face was red as a beet and sweat was rolling down the sides of her face. She was cursing Dick under her breath. "That son-of-a-bitch! He is so lucky I didn't have to see him before we left. I know I would have bitch-slapped him but good. And probably more than once. And I would have probably kicked him in the balls to boot"! I sat in total silence as she let it all out. I had been there and done that too many times myself already. She caught herself and looked at me and apologized for her rant, but said she meant every word of it. I understood completely. Rachel went to take a shower as I took care of the pets and checked my email. It was only minutes later that I heard Rachel belting out more expletives towards Dick. She came out of the bathroom dripping wet wrapped in a towel. "Holy shit! Look at my legs"! I gasped as I saw Rachel's legs swollen so badly from her knees to her feet. She had spent the last three days driving nearly non-stop for 12-14 hours straight with very little movement of her legs that had been hanging down off the bench seat of the truck. "I have damn elephantitis of the legs", she screamed! She jumped on her bed and as she stacked pillow after pillow to elevate her feet she looked at me and said, "It's time to bring out those special brownies you brought from California". I think it was our best night of sleep since the trip began.

Each morning we were on the road before sunrise and didn't settle into another hotel until after sunset. On day four Rachel and I had a "moment" after traveling for a few hours. She needed me to tell her the exact name or number of the exit we needed to take and thought I had. But it wasn't clear enough for her on the signs and the traffic was horrible and we missed the exit. It took us awhile to get back to where we needed to be. Precious time was lost. I was upset. She was upset. But we both knew it was no one's fault and we were upset only because we were both so tired at this point. That damn beast was beginning to close in around us and we both had cabin fever. We were quiet for awhile and let it go. This was to be our only "moment" the entire trip. On this same day we somehow got off at the wrong exit again and found ourselves on a flat, completely desolate road for a very long time before we realized we were going the wrong way. There weren't very many road signs and once we realized we were heading in the wrong direction, Rachel began getting nervous about the gas getting low and the fact that she could not find a side of the road that looked safe enough to turn The Beast around. We finally came upon an area that looked safe enough and looked like it would not cause us to get stuck in the sand. Eventually we saw a sign that pointed us in the right direction. A few cars were now on the road with us. But there were no gas stations in sight. All of sudden I realized I had to use the bathroom really bad. Well, Rachel suggested, being the camper and road traveler she was, that she would just pull over and I could pee outside on the side of the road. Well, I was having none of that I'm here to tell you. It would be our luck that a cop would pass just as I dropped my drawers and I would be arrested for indecent exposure or something. So then she suggested I use the dog's small, plastic water bowl and just pee in the cab of the truck. I am sure the look I gave her was one she will never forget. But she toughened up on me and said it was either that or pee my pants!

Now the next few moments were a memory maker for sure. There we were in the middle of nowhere in broad daylight in a crowded truck cab filled with three animals and everything else we had and I had to try and somehow get my pants down and pee in a very small plastic bowl. All this while trying not to be seen by passersby and heaven forbid, not spilling a drop. Now keep in mind that I had absolutely no floorboard room whatsoever as I had set up one of the dog's beds there and had the cooler at my feet as well. This is probably why I never got elephantitis of the legs like Rachel because I had to keep my feet up on the dashboard the whole time. Well, I am proud to say I was successful, even though Rachel was giggling the whole time and I was cursing up a storm. I didn't spill a drop... until... Well, when I tried to empty the bowl out the window a huge gust of wind came up and splattered my pee all over the place; my hand, my arm, the outside of the door and the window too. And I hadn't even been able at this point to pull my damn pants back up since both my hands were holding a full bowl of pee and trying not to spill any of it! And the dogs were all over me even though Rachel had tried to hold them back. The more she laughed the more excited they became and she couldn't keep them back. Rachel was laughing her ass off and trying her best to control the dogs. At this point I had no choice but to join her in laughter. And I am pleased to say that even though we did not run out of gas nor did I get caught with my pants down, but once we finally made it to a gas station Rachel admitted that she had peed her pants a little from laughing at me so hard. "Karma is a bitch," I said as she jumped out of the truck so fast and ran towards the restrooms at top speed. She tripped slightly jumping the curb near the front doors of the convenience store and I laughed even harder when I saw she almost lost her flip-flop doing so. I am sure she didn't see the bikers on the side watching this nearly six foot tall woman running at mach speed to get to the bathroom. Although I am sure they knew exactly why she was running like that. It was a funny sight to see a grown woman running with her legs nearly crossed as she did. She did not hold it against me upon her return when I was still laughing and trying to describe to her what she looked like when she exited the truck so quickly.

The last couple of days were very long and I thought we would never hit the east coast states. Poor Rachel's legs would only decrease in swelling just slightly overnight from being elevated, but would immediately swell up again within a couple of hours being in the truck. As we neared the end of our journey we obviously couldn't go without a final "hitch" on the last few miles.

It was already dark, Rachel had less than four hours before

she had to catch her plane back to Florida. There was major rush hour traffic and the interstate was packed and here we come hauling butt right into the middle of it. The signs were too numerous and confusing and before we knew it we were mistakenly headed straight into Dulles Airport driving this huge, bright yellow diesel truck. I got on the phone with my brother and told him he would have to come meet us somewhere outside the airport and lead us out of this madness and to the house. Then we saw the sign that we didn't want to see. In huge, bold letters, "No trucks allowed". Rachel was heading for the arrival area where people who had just arrived were being picked up. We were trapped with no way to turn around and had no choice but to plow ever so cautiously and slowly through this highly secured airport just miles from our nations' capital. Again, more signs everywhere stating "no trucks allowed". We just knew that we had been spotted by security cameras and before we knew it we would probably be surrounded by gun-wielding military and security personnel screaming at us to stop and get out of the truck slowly with our hands raised! I just knew that they would think the truck was filled with explosives and we were terrorists. And I am quite sure the intimidating shadows of Edward and Carlisle behind us didn't help. Rachel began praying out loud so fast I almost peed my pants laughing again. "This is so not funny", she said all the while laughing herself. Well thanks be to God we managed to get out of that airport without being arrested or shot. We spotted my brother and he led us out of there. Within a few miles we were in front of the entrance to the beautiful community that was to be my new home. Rachel exited the truck and let my brother drive it through the maze-like parking lot and he parked The Beast once and for all.

Within a few minutes of arriving and getting the animals and ourselves into the house, it was time for Rachel to get her belongings organized and ready to head back to the airport to go home. We ate a snack and "toured" the house. It was everything and more. The pictures my brother had sent me did not do it justice. I loved it. Rachel changed clothes and freshened up, still in pain from how swollen her legs were and how tight the skin was pulling. She downed a "special brownie" and we left for the airport. It was so bittersweet saying goodbye to her now after all we had been though the last few days. We were both leaning into each other with exhaustion as we hugged and cried. I told her I would never be able to find the words of gratitude I felt for all she had done for me and driving us across country like she did. She once again held my face in her hands, looked me straight in the eye and said, "You do not need any words whatsoever Hon, and I would do it all over again if I had to". Rachel would be coming back in a couple of months to go the Twilight Breaking Dawn Part I movie premier with me. This time her trip will once again be for fun and pleasure. The house would be all complete by then with my furniture and décor mixed with my brother's beautiful things as well. As I watched her walk away I took several deep breaths, wiped away my tears, and turned around to start my new life.

Upon arriving back to the townhome, I realized I was home. I talked with Tom about where I thought certain furniture and décor should go. I had several nice antique pieces that belonged to our Grandmother and Mother. Warm and fuzzy is how I would describe it. My brother is happy and makes me feel right at home. I too feel happy. It has been a long time since I had that feeling.

WTF?

It is Friday night and the first weekend in my new home. My brother is at his cottage on the Bay for the weekend. I have been taking the dogs each evening for their last walk around 9pm before bed. After our walk, I went upstairs to watch TV and slip into bed for the night. I checked my messages and saw that a call came in from his office in California at 9:45pm. I thought it was strange that he would not call me from his cell. I decided to ignore it and turned off the light and fell into a deep sleep. I awoke to my phone ringing at 11:40pm. I answered immediately thinking it could be one of my sons or my brother. The person on the other end of the phone was ranting and screeching and making no sense at all. At first I thought it was my neighbor in California drunk dialing me until I asked a few questions and realized that's not who it was. I asked, "Who is this"? She yelled her name at me, "It's Puki". Oh dear God it is her! It was like being in the Twilight Zone; I couldn't explain it if I had to.

She was screaming at me, "You stealer"! "You know what you did"! "You don't want to mess with me"! And she ranted on and on and on. I hung up on her three times and she called back immediately every time. Finally at midnight I just turned off my phone. At 3am I woke up and she had called three more times and left a voice mail. Of course I had it archived so I could keep it case she continued to harass me. Then I would have recorded proof should I ever need to pursue a lawsuit against her nasty ass.

To this day I have no idea what pissed her off so much that she had to call and harass me. It did my heart good to know she was really upset and I have no idea why nor do I care. As I fell into slumber I smiled and drifted off to the best night's sleep in months!

Of course he got his way like I thought. He moved back into the house three days after I left. He had it painted, bought new furniture, and moved in lock, stock, and barrel. I hope he is happy sitting in the house all alone with his liquor. He had this planned from the beginning; he knew I would leave and he was bound and determined to move his ass back in.

I still miss living in California, especially the weather. I'm getting adjusted to living back in Virginia. I miss my west coast friends and the places I frequented. Now I can make new memories without him. I can honestly say from the bottom of my heart I am ready to do that. In the beginning it wasn't even an option. I didn't feel complete if I wasn't with him. I have come a long way since then. My life does go on without him.

Have you ever had a dream and woke up to realize that all the negative things that you lived with for so long are now gone? This is how I feel. I can't explain it; it just feels right, where before it didn't.

I sent one more email to his office asking him to put her on a leash! I'm sure he didn't know she called me eight times and the last message was a voice mail with obscenities. Three hours later I received the most hateful email from him; or was it really him? I know he didn't write this. I hope he didn't anyway, after all the years in college his grammar is better than the email I received. It went on and on about we should have divorced earlier, he was with his new family and friends and I was nothing to him. He referred to me as "your sorry self". I know him better than this and I know how she speaks. SHE wrote this from his work email. Guess we know who calls the shots and wears the pants.

I wanted to respond, but neither of them are worth my time and effort. I just want it all to stop once and for all. He is nothing to me anymore. I never thought it would get to this; I can honestly say any love that I felt is gone. I finally found the switch and flipped it to off. He was exhausting; it just took me a long time to realize it.

Family and friends have been there for me from the beginning. I don't think I could do what I've done without their support and love.

It's been almost three weeks since the nasty email from "him". I believe in my heart he did not write that message. Still, I feel no emotions about him. That's when you know it's in the past, when you feel nothing. No hate, anger, regret, love, and definitely no tears. I try and remember back to the good times. However, the past three years over shadow everything that was good. I feel so much more at peace with everything since we split.

I always said a lot of my health problems were because of him it was true. I feel better than I have in years.

Moving on

The house has come together so nicely. All the furniture fits perfectly and the décor items are all in place. I really feel at home here and I know this was the right decision and move for me.

I spent the last couple of days completing applications for holiday help at the lovely Town Center a mile away from home. It will be good to get out and mingle with people again now that I am settled into the house, finding my way around the area and have time on my hands. I am in such a better place than I was last year at this time. Our lives can change in a second when we least expect it. Sometimes through death, relocation, loss of a job or loved one, or when your spouse decides he/she is done being married and wants to separate, moving on isn't always easy; especially when you get to be a certain age. Stability is something of the past. These are different times for everyone and none of us can predict what will come to us at any given moment.

Putting the pieces of our lives back is the hard part; that's where we rely on the ones we can trust and depend on to be there for us. I could not imagine what I have gone through these past years if I had to do it alone. I am stronger and a better person today because of the people that were there for me during this time.

I miss my girls in California. Even though we talk almost every day, I miss seeing them. Even if it was just to say hello or go to dance class, there was that comfortable interaction I have to now create with new people.

I was never big on Christmas, especially after the boys were grown. I remember from my childhood my parents drinking too much, having a fight and the tree toppling over more years than not. I would lie in bed and wonder how Santa would come to our house since the tree was on the floor and all the ornaments were broken. I would cry myself to sleep only to wake up and it was all back together. To this day I never figured out how they made it all happen, but they did. Santa would always come and drop off the presents.

I just never understood why people would go into debt and through all the stress of making sure presents were bought for all the right people and equally among the kids. Heaven forbid one kid get more than another. Call me Scrooge, but it just didn't make sense. The entire meaning of Christmas has turned to nothing but a materialistic nightmare. The stores advertise Christmas before Halloween; it just wasn't fun anymore.

Thanksgiving is my favorite holiday and time of the year, it always has been. I remember waking up to a cold, overcast day with the smell of turkey in the house along with pumpkin pies, chocolate chip cookies, and all the goodies that complement the entire feast. We would always have a big breakfast and then watch the Macy's Thanksgiving Day parade on TV. Every year at 4pm we would sit at the table with all the fine china and silverware eating until we couldn't eat another thing. The day was full of family and friends. There were no presents. It was a time to get together and give thanks for your blessings. This is something everyone needs to do. If we wake up every morning we need to be thankful; it sure as hell beats the alternative!

This year Thanksgiving will be spent at the cottage on the Bay with Tom. Other than my kids not being there it will be just as I remembered from years past. Tom's lady friend and her boys will join us and it will be a happy day.

My life seems to be peaceful and relaxed for now. I pinch myself every day. Everyone should take a moment and think... is this where I am supposed to be?

It may snow in October and be 100-plus degrees in June, being back on the east coast is so much better for me in mind, body, and spirit, then staying in California right now. All my good memories came to a halt in 2008. If it hadn't been for the people I met living on the west coast it would have been unbearable.

I am as happy as I can be; we make our own happiness and I think I'm making mine. It sure as hell is better than it was two years ago. I was just going through the motions and didn't even realize it. I was a slave to being there for him. Maybe I didn't support him the way he expected with his work. How could I? There were way too many secrets and she made sure I was kept out of the loop as to what was going on in the office. It was only going to get worse and never better. He just didn't see it or maybe he didn't care.

I now sleep through the night and wake up in a good mood every morning. It is comforting living in a home again; not just a big empty cold house.

Missing my Gal-pals

There isn't a day that goes by I don't miss my girlfriends. They were my backbone during these past couple of years. I spent more time with them than with Dick! I miss driving over at a moment's notice if one of us needed something. Just going to a movie or watching TV together was comforting. I miss the folks at my favorite restaurant and I miss my dance classes. I had so many good times during the years I lived there. I'm still in my healing process. I still have a lot to give, and I plan to do just that as soon as I am ready.

Rachel will be visiting Friday November 18th so we can go see the Twilight Saga - Breaking Dawn, Part 1 movie together. We promised wherever we lived we would see this together. We are like a couple of teenagers. I am a Twi-Hard Team Carlisle one hundred percent and proud of it! Rachel is Team Edward all the way. My office is a shrine to the Twilight Saga. We all have our means of "guilty pleasures" and Twilight is one of mine. It makes me smile and go to a place that is make believe and forget everything else going on around me. I feel like I know all the characters personally. Anyone that is a true Twi-Hard knows where I'm coming from. It will be good to see Rachel. I love and miss our girl time together. And this visit is for the good stuff this time. We will laugh until we cry and swoon over the Twilight movie. Even though I talk, text, and email everyday with my girlfriends, it isn't the same as having them close to hold your hand or lend that shoulder when times are tough. Rachel and I are sure we will squeal and cry during the much-anticipated wedding scenes. We will probably hold hands and sigh at the beauty of it all.

It's the week before Thanksgiving and I started my first day working part time at a clothing boutique at the Towne Center. I survived my first "Black Friday" experience and every bone in my body can attest to that.

It will be good for me to be out and around people since the Christmas holidays are not my favorite time of the year and this year will be a little more difficult for sure. I got a little weepy the other night and my brother, bless his soul, said, "There will be no crying in this house"! I needed to hear that. I stopped crying immediately.

Will it Ever End With Him?

It wasn't enough that his skanky business partner called and harassed me late at night, then I get the "good-bye" email from him, or was it her? I got his message loud and clear. Before I left I gave him a piece of advice. I told him to watch his back because no one liked him and no one wanted to see him back in the house without me. Anyone that was close to me knew the whole sordid story and he lost a lot of friends after everything came out. Dick never had many friends to begin with, only acquaintances and business associates. All our friends were in fact MY friends who only befriended him through me. He said many times he envied how people liked and gravitated towards me. He said I was like a beacon of light that just drew everyone in when I entered a room. He always asked me why everyone loved me so much; for some reason that bothered him. I had something he didn't. It was called being human and treating people with respect. He didn't have that.

At some point in time after I moved he received a "disturbing letter" thinking it was from me. He called my friend after having a few shots of whatever his drink of choice is nowadays. She just so happened to be back in Sausalito to visit her daughter. He wanted to know if she delivered a letter for me. She had no idea what he was talking about. Marlo called me early the next morning to ask me about the letter he was talking about and to tell me about his drunken phone call. I know nothing about any letter. He isn't worth me sending him squat!

Thanksgiving eve and Dick sends me a text saying he isn't going to pay me anymore spousal support because I continue to harass him with letters. I think he has a screw loose; the curtains are blowing and the windows are shut! On my trip across country he had sent an email that made no sense at all. For someone that went to college so much and obtained all those degrees, he sure has become brain dead! Or maybe the alcohol has turned him into a raving lunatic now.

He is now two payments late. I had to call my attorney so she could file the paperwork against him for failure to pay spousal support. He has to know there will be consequences to his idiotic actions. Like I said, he isn't acting like a person that gives a damn. I am sure Puki has told him to not give me another dime. I don't know which of the two of them is more stupid!

I am going to let my attorney take care of him, he isn't worth my time. He wants to be in control like he has for the past sixteen years. Well not anymore, I am done letting this so-called "man" call the shots. Let the judge call the shots now! Judges don't look too kindly on men who don't pay their court-ordered spousal support or child support. Especially after their ex-wife so graciously signs away the house to them and leaves their business alone.

The Holidays

Our lovely Christmas tree is up and it is only November 29th! I haven't had a tree in years. In the past I could just shut my eyes and wake up January 1st and it would be fine with me. My brother and I are hosting a Holiday Open House; it will be fun to meet all his work folks. It was a chance to dress up and be festive. I haven't done that in a while. Dick was never a big fan of any of the holidays. I tried to make it nice for us; always decorating the house, baked Christmas cookies, cooked or we would go over and have dinner with Marlo's family. All he ever wanted to do for the past three years was work.

My youngest son and daughter-in-law came to visit for a few days. It was so good to see them. It has only been about three months since we last saw each other and their timing was perfect. We laughed so much our faces hurt. It was the best medicine anyone could ask for.

Marlo is coming for a visit on Christmas day. I can't wait to see her. We have plans to do all the things we enjoy; the best part is hanging out together and catching up. It never gets old.

Dick told Marlo in that drunken phone call weeks ago that I couldn't let go. But I had actually unconsciously let go the day he walked into that office. I just stuck with it and fought for something that was a losing battle to begin with. Things were never the same. It was sixteen years I'll never get back. Yes I'm hurt; my world was turned upside down. But now I see that it has turned upside down for the better!

One of my favorite things to say is, "There was life before him and there is life after him".

A Few More Things

Its three weeks shy of a year since I started writing my story. At first it was just notes on paper, a journal of thoughts and memories. It became therapeutic for me to write down my emotions on paper. I know there are many stories like mine and a lot worse. I came from a generation when you left home, you went to college, got married, and raised a family. That life was through rose-colored glasses; it doesn't always work that way.

If nothing else, I hope my story will help anyone that faces a similar situation and finds themselves asking, "What do I do now"? "Where do I go"? "How will I pay my rent and bills"? "What about the pets, the house"? "I have to leave my friends and family and the city I came to love so much". "Who can help me answer these questions"? It is a scary, dark place to be. Some people take to drinking or doing drugs, some find themselves homeless. It doesn't have to be that way. Know who your true friends are and ask your family for help. They are there for us as we are there for them.

It's been a rough couple of years. I spoke earlier about the seven stages of grief and I find myself at a place trying to reconstruct ME and my life. The last is Acceptance. I can honestly say I am not there yet. Life is way too short to sit and dwell. I am finally seeing the light at the end of the tunnel and I am sure 2012 will be a much better year than 2011. As a matter of fact I KNOW it will be. I am stronger and am starting to get myself assurance back one day at a time.

It's Christmas Eve; tonight is all about family. Going to a traditional dinner at our cousin's home with lots of children, grandchildren, and my aunt, who is now the matriarch of our family. It will be good to see and meet new family members. As I sat and listened to all the chatter and stories it gave me a feeling of warmth and comfort being surrounded by family members again.

Christmas Day 2011. My brother, his lady and myself shared a quiet Christmas morning opening gifts with the smell of the burning fire and the beauty of the tree. It made me realize what I had missed over the years. Even though I wasn't a big fan of the holiday, this year was different.

This New Years I spent in Florida with my son, daughter-in-law, grandchildren, my BFF Rachel and her son. I cherished it more than New Years' in the past, even as we sat on the couch watching The Smurfs Movie with the kids! It made me thankful for all the love I have in my life. I can feel it; I am a better person today because of the love that surrounds me.

Out With the Past and Into the Future

I'm back at my brother's cottage on the Chesapeake Bay where a little over a year ago I started writing my story. It seemed fitting to come and finish it on the Bay. As I sit here looking at the snow falling, the bay is hardly visible and it's a breathtaking sheet of white. It is one of the most peaceful places to finish what has been a therapeutic, eye-opening journey for me.

If my story helps one other man or woman going through a life changing experience like mine, then I'll feel like I have accomplished what I set out to do in writing and publishing my story.

It is now into the first week of January 2012. My old life is over and I am ready to file it away and start again. The saying goes, "What doesn't kill will make us stronger". I believe this to be true. I am in a much better place now than I was a year ago. The tears have stopped and I don't question,

"Why me"? My heart isn't heavy anymore. Whether or not I'll ever fall in love again is an answer I don't have at the moment. Only time will tell.

There are several things I know now that came from the past few years of going through my own private hell. Do we really know the person we are with? It is safe to say nothing lasts forever and if you want something in life you have to make it happen yourself. It will take time and work but we are responsible for our destiny. Most importantly let your family and friends be there for you and don't be afraid to ask for their help. Believe in yourself and keep faith.

I have more years behind me than in front of me and I plan to make the rest of my life as fulfilling as I can. I am doing just that.

I can honestly say I left my heart in San Francisco, and not because of him. I fell in love with the city way before Dick came into my life. It was with much sadness I had to leave the place I called home for sixteen years.

The most difficult part of moving forward with my life is that there was never closure to why it turned out the way it did. "It just isn't working anymore" was the coward's way out. I never thought of him as a coward before. Now it is just one more adjective to describe the man he is now, not the man he was.

Someone asked me recently if I have forgiven him for what he put me through? My response was, "What he put me through isn't worthy of my forgiveness", not now, maybe someday. The saying goes, "Time heals all wounds"... does it?

The End

They Teach It at Stanford, by Sharon Rose

from the March 2011 newsletter of
The Business & Professional Women of Nevada County

They Teach It at Stanford

In a recent evening class at Stanford there was a lecture on the mind-body connection - the relationship between stress and disease. The speaker was the head of psychiatry at Stanford and said, among other things, that one of the best things that a man could do for his health is to be married to a woman whereas for a woman, one of the best things she could do for her health was to nurture her relationships with her girlfriends. Women connect with each other differently and provide support systems that help each other to deal with stress and difficult life experiences. Physically this quality "girlfriend time" helps us to create more serotonin - a neurotransmitter that helps combat depression and can create a general feeling of well-being. Women share feelings whereas men often form relationships around activities.

Men rarely sit down with a buddy and talk about how they feel about certain things or how their personal lives are going. Women do it all of the time. We share from our souls with our sisters/mothers, and evidently that is very good for our health. He said that spending time with a friend is just as important to our general health as jogging or working out at a gym. So every time you hang out to schmooze with a gal pal, just pat yourself on the back and congratulate yourself for doing something good for your health! We are indeed very, very lucky. So let's toast to our friendship with our girlfriends.

A special mention to the women that have been there for me during this heartbreaking and healing time. Each of these wonderful ladies has been an inspiration and true friend to me. Each is completely different in every way, shape and form! Their friendship goes above and beyond. I am blessed to know them and feel their love and support now and always. I pray that other people are as blessed to find such amazing, true friends.

Ms. D

Thank you for everything you do! Not just for me but all the students, young and old, that you have given the confidence and strength to excel through life. You made Wednesdays and Thursdays something I looked forward to. I hadn't danced in a long time until I started at your studio. It was something I always loved doing and now it meant so much more. You helped these old bones get strong again and you gave me back the confidence I was losing. It was my time just for two nights a week and I loved it! Through dancing I met such wonderful people and watched them grow into young men and women, get married and have babies; all this in only six years. Just think of all the lives you touched. When I meet people I tell them proudly I dance at WCDT Studio and they say, "Oh, I know Ms. D". You are an institution in the community. Thank goodness for Facebook, we can post pictures and chat and we won't let 3,000 miles stop us. As long as there is a WCDT performance I will be in the audience smiling as the dancers take the stage. You are a special friend and mentor and I will miss you when I leave, but promise to always stay in touch. You are a very special lady! I am proud to call you my friend.

Peg

What can I say? They broke the mold with you. There is no one like you in the entire world. Girl, I will never forget our first meeting. I knew from the firm handshake we would be friends forever. We share so many of the same means of entertainment: TV, movies and theatre and our love of Regis. I have enjoyed every venture we have been on together from New York to Beverly Hills and hopefully there will be many more down the road. I always loved when we would get together. You always had several sheets of "notes" you had jotted down while watching TV or reading the paper. We would talk endlessly about different TV shows we both enjoyed watching. We loved discussing the beautiful gowns on the red carpet before the award shows. No one enjoyed our favorite bottle of Gloria champagne more than we did. Remember our HFC events, our parties and nights out with RS! Way too many Cosmos! We won't see as much of each other but will always be in touch. I expect you to come visit me when I get settled. There are two bar stools at the Mayflower Hotel in Washington, DC that have our names on them! You will always be family to me. I can now use your famous phrase, "party of one, please"! I am proud to call you my friend.

Simone

Talk about strength! I think you have given me more than I realize. Without going into your own personal tragedy I think you are the strongest of all the ladies. I hope your guidance will carry me through. When they gave out friends I was lucky enough to meet you. I can remember the first time we met at the insurance office in Pleasanton, CA. I thought, "Now that's a lady to respect"! She is my kind a gal. So many laughs we've shared, so many good times, so many condoms (private joke), serving brunch on the yachts,

I could go on and on. My favorite time together was the Christmas party at the San Francisco Zoo Lion House. We will never forget that night! Somehow I understood how that tiger wound up in the hotel room from the movie "The Hangover" (another private joke). What happens at the zoo stays at the zoo! I know we were honored as your friends when you asked us to be your matron of honor and best man when you married Bobby on New Year's Eve 2005 at City Hall in San Francisco. You are a rare beauty inside and out, tough as nails and soft as silk. You will always be in my heart pretty lady. I am proud to call you my friend.

Marlo

Lord Jesus what can I say. Two peas in a pod. Two Libras who think so much alike. When I fall apart who will be over in five minutes to pick me up? I will miss our happy and sad girl times; there were so many this past year. You are the one that has made me step outside my box and look at everything in a different light, even when I didn't want to leave the box. The positive energy you bring to the table could light up an entire city block. I could be crying my eyes out and you were right by my side making me see there was light at the end of the long, dark tunnel. Thanks to your love and support I indeed see there is in fact light at the end of the tunnel. You were also someone I knew would be with me forever. At this time of our lives we are both expanding on new journeys; some people would never make the attempt. We have done it before and we can do it again. I know you will excel in whatever path you follow, as will I. No matter where we live we will always be as close as we are now. I love you my friend! It's because of you I write my book. I am so proud to call you my friend.

Addison

Oh my how many years…34! It would take another book to write of our experiences. Mine couldn't be published though until I've passed! You are the only one of the ladies that knows the husbands. We have been through more than I have with anyone, good and bad. I watched you become a mother to Marie and Richard; we were maid of honors in each other's weddings. Who did I call every time I needed someone to watch the boys while we got called to the ER for mom or my number one son? We were there together to bury our moms not to mention all the other heartaches we went through in between. We tackled some of the wildest nights I can remember. My favorite was the night I parked my Mustang on the front steps and my son came out and asked why the car was not parked in the driveway? I do believe we were together that night! Who knew 34 years ago we would be where we are today? You have been my heart and soul, never judging me once in all those years. Your day is coming, this setback you've lived with the past five years will pass. You will make that happen. We are both survivors. My back is stronger because you stand behind it. When they gave out BFF's they gave me you. I love you forever. I am so very proud to call you my friend.

Rachel

I was working at a company in Tampa, Florida. It was 22 years ago I caught a glimpse of this tall, blonde beauty at work with a Georgia peach accent walking down the hall. I knew that moment we would be bound together for life. You have been like a sister and daughter I never had and one of the best friends anyone could ever ask for. We have been through some times together I have never shared with anyone but you. We have cried and laughed more together than I can count. There hasn't been a time when you weren't there for me. We are more than friends; soul mates might describe it better. We know what the other is thinking before the words come out. I watched you become an amazing mother to Luke. If anyone deserves that title it is you. Then there is the Twilight Saga! None of the other ladies share the way we feel about this phenomena. There isn't a day that goes by that I don't thank God you are in my life. Without going into detail with all you've been through, and you have been through hell and back, you are one of the strongest women I know. Never change from that Georgia peach I met in Tampa over two decades ago. I look forward to our journey driving across country together; we never do anything that doesn't end in a good time! When you retire and we tour the country in your motorhome, "Thelma and Louise II" will be painted on the side (along with a scene from Twilight I'm sure). I will love you as long as there is breath in my body and I will always be there for you. I am so very proud you are my friend.

Thank you ladies for being my friends and touching my life now and forever. Everyone should be as lucky to have the friendship we've shared through the years. I love each one of you more than you'll know!! If I had to choose one of my ladies over a husband, each one of you would win hands down.

About the Author

First time author Carlie Peters, resides on the east coast with her brother and pets. She is currently working on her second book, a follow up to her first. She works part time, volunteers and enjoys traveling to visit her three grown sons and their families along with spending time with her closest friends.

www.ingramcontent.com/pod-product-compliance
Lightning Source LLC
Chambersburg PA
CBHW021600280526
45784CB00001BA/437